Pens for Peace

edited by
Noel Flannery & Matt Cannon

Irish Peace Institute Ltd., 2001

Published in 2001 by
Irish Peace Institute
University of Limerick
Limerick, Ireland
phone: 061-202768
fax: 061-202572
http://www.ul.ie/ipi

ISBN   1-874653-64-X

Printed by
Limerick Printing
Killmallock Road Ind. Estate
Killmallock Road
Limerick

Cover Photo
Courtesy of Comstock Images
http://www.comstock.com/

Come - pledge again thy heart and hand -
One grasp that ne'er shall sever;
Our watchword be - "Our native land"-
Our motto - "Love for ever".
And let the Orange lily be
Thy badge, my patriot brother -
The everlasting Green for me;
And we for one another.

Behold how green the gallant stem
On which the flower is blowing;
How in one heavenly breeze and beam
Both flower and stem are glowing.
The same good soil, sustaining both,
Makes both united flourish;
But cannot give the Orange growth,
And cease the Green to nourish.

Yea, more - the hand that plucks the flower
Will vainly strive to cherish;
The stem blooms on - but in that hour
The flower begins to perish.
Regard them, then, of equal worth
While lasts their genial weather;
The time's at hand when into earth
The two shall sink together.

Ev'n thus be, in our country's cause,
Our party feelings blended;
Till lasting peace, from equal laws,
On both shall have descended.
Till then the Orange lily be
Thy badge, my patriot brother -
The everlasting Green for me;
And - we for one another.

John D. Fraser 1809-1849

Preface

The Irish Peace Institute was founded in 1984 on the initiative of Dr. Brendan O'Regan and with the co-operation of the University of Limerick, the University of Ulster and Co-operation Ireland.

It is a non-governmental, non-political, and not-for-profit organisation funded by the EU Peace & Reconciliation Programme, private and corporate donors; incorporated as a company limited by guarantee and accorded charitable status by the Revenue Commissioners.

The mission of the Irish Peace Institute is to contribute to the process of peace-building through programmes of education, research and outreach directed to the development of mutual understanding and co-operation between the people of Northern Ireland and the Republic of Ireland.

Noel Flannery

Noel Flannery is an Hon. Commerce graduate with an M. Econ. Sc. from University College Dublin, and an H.Dip. Ed. from University College Cork. He was a part-time lecturer with University College Cork and the University of Limerick. Noel served as a Member of the Governing Body of the Limerick Institute of Technology while lecturing full-time as a member of staff. He has worked in industry in the United Kingdom and with the Revenue Commissioners in Ireland. An activist with the Irish Peace Institute since 1993, he is Chairman of the Institute's Outreach Committee and a Member of the Board. He is a developer and property owner in Limerick.

Matt Cannon

Matthew Cannon B.A., Ph.D. is originally from New York. He received a Bachelor of Arts from Syracuse University in International Relations/Political Science in 1994. In 2001 he received a Ph.D. from the University of Limerick for his study of the role of local governments in the formation of the Transmanche Euroregion across the English Channel. He writes extensively on cross-border co-operation, policing and developments in the role of local government. He helped found the *University of Limerick Political & Economic Review*, now known as *Perspectives*, and also acted as editor of the journal. He currently resides in Limerick, Ireland where he is employed by the Irish Peace Institute.

Acknowledgements

A publication such as this is the result of the work of many different people. It would not have been possible without the input and support of the contributers. We would also like to name a few people who contributed a great deal of time and energy to the project. Like the glue that holds these pages together, Dorothy Cantrell kept the project moving along swiftly. Tracey Gleeson provided sound advice and input into many aspects of the publication. Finally Una Heaton offered artistic input and support in the design and layout of the publication.

Introduction

Pens for Peace draws inspiration from the often quoted line, *"the pen is mightier than the sword"*. We decided to put this adage to the test by offering a forum for authors to air their views on peace. Through debate which might arise from the contributions contained in this publication we can develop and promote understanding, and it is only through understanding one another that we can truly achieve peace.

We hope the range of articles in this book is a source for multi-cultural distilling and blending. Diversity, rightly understood in this context, is wealth; it helps us to change and grow by selling what is good in our culture and buying what is good in other cultures. We can benefit by distilling the best from each culture and by combining we get strength and synergy from each.

We, as editors, wanted to interpose ourselves as little as possible between the writers and readers. We believe this publication to be a source of new ideas and a useful tool to stimulate debate. Our purpose was to provide a snapshot of ideas and opinions on the notion of *'peace'* at a specific point in time.

In compiling the essays contained in this book we approached over a hundred people whom we believed could provide a valuable insight into the subject of peace. We understand some were not able to participate in the project due to their demanding schedules, and we appreciate the regret expressed by those who declined to participate. We would like to thank the participants who were able to meet our tight time constraints and contribute to a collection which we believe will provide an interesting watermark in the history of peace making.

Noel Flannery & Matt Cannon
Editors

Contents

The Fabric of Peace

Fraser Agnew

Fraser Agnew a Ph.D. graduate is an acknowledged authority on the Battle of the Diamond and the formation of the Orange Order. He travels extensively to lecture on these subjects as well as the Williamite wars and the Industrial Revolution. Well known in Unionist politics, Fraser is a member and former mayor of Newtownabbey Borough Council and currently Chairman of the Ulster Tourist Development Association. A 54 year old researcher and writer, he is married with one son and is a qualified soccer coach. At many of the junior soccer grounds in the province he is a familiar and respected figure as he reports on games as a part-time soccer journalist.

A friend of the writer has been heavily involved in conflict resolution work in Moldova and while holding discussions in the disputed territory of Transdniestra, an elderly woman commented on community development work saying, "We don't really want to know about jobs and economic recovery and all of those things; all we want is peace. Can you not help us bring an end to this war? We want peace, but we don't want their flag, or their languages or to be Romanians".

The last sentence in particular should be of interest to us all because it indicates that the most difficult conflict facing mankind is not those that take place across borders or boundaries but rather internal frontiers.

Whether it is the Middle East, the Balkans, Eastern Europe or Northern Ireland, the fact is that where differing racial, ethnic or religious groups compete for the same territory, then the real divisions lie within the minds of ordinary people.

1

The ideal of a pluralist peace for a pluralist people is a commendable one, but realistically it has also been the cause of much strife, conflict and division. A cloth woven from different threads can be an attractive proposition but unless woven carefully, it will inevitably unravel. All of the strands must be compatible to ensure a perfect product.

The current peace process in Northern Ireland is one such poorly woven cloth - indeed many important strands are missing. Despite some skillful spinning by two Governments and pro-Agreement supporters, the process lacks at least 30% of the necessary material (i.e. at least half of the unionist population) to make it a perfect piece of cloth.

In ideal conflict resolution terms, it is always preferable that no one should be excluded from the process, for experience shows that by denying the force of argument there is a risk of it being replaced by the argument of force. Thus, it is imperative that all agents approach and participate in the process on equal terms and enjoy equal status within it.

In Northern Ireland, violence has created a power-bargaining process where those on the wrong end of the violence will see many of their rights eroded. This is certainly the case in the Protestant community where there is much frustration caused through the perception that violence pays.

The Protestant community is increasingly marginalised by the wider political developments. There is a growing insecurity and lack of confidence in its own position which is reflected by its reluctance to embrace cross-community contact.

Protestants do not feel they have any ownership of the Peace Process and that it fails to satisfy their identity needs, yet in an identity-related conflict, symbols are probably more important in satisfying identity needs than political, social and economic issues - hence the comments of the elderly people in Transdniestra and hence the difficulties with the process in Northern Ireland.

Politicians and commentators from outside Northern Ireland have always had pre-decided ideas about what is necessary for the Province without even bothering to consult the people most interested.

Those who are divorced from reality because of their position in society should not enforce their views on others on the basis that what they believe appears to be an ideal situation.

It is those at the grassroots who suffer the most in a conflict situation but they probably lack the authority or even the responsibility or resources to resolve that conflict.

While it is up to the political leadership to resolve the conflict on the basis that they have authority to do so, they must accurately reflect the fears and aspirations which give rise to the conflict within their respective communities. Unlike Nationalists and Republicans, some Unionist leadership have consistently failed to represent and even recognise the fears and aspirations of its community.

It is this that has created a power-bargaining process. There is a lack of confidence in the process creating suspicion, political and violent reaction.

History shows that where there is internal conflict, political and military attempts to force a resolution to conflicts, such as exists in Northern Ireland, invariably fail and even intensify them.

A win-win situation, as opposed to one community achieving victory over the other, is a desirable ideal. Unfortunately, in Northern Ireland the process is not inclusive, there is little understanding, particularly of the Unionist and Protestant position, and while the process continues to exclude democrats, peace will be a mere cry with war the reality.

A Lasting Peace in Ireland

Bertie Ahern

Bertie Aheran was educated at St Aidan's CBS, Whitehal; Rathmines College of Commerce, UCD and the London School of Economics. Qualified as an accountant before entering the Dáil in the Fianna Fáil landslide of 1977. He was appointed as Assistant Government Whip in 1980 and Chief Whip in March 1982. He held various opposition front bench appointments in the mid-1980s before entering cabinet as Minister for Labour on the return of Fianna Fáil to government in 1987. He was a member of Dublin City Council from 1979-1991, being elected Lord Mayor in 1986. He survived the fall of the Haughey government and was promoted Minister for Finance under Albert Reynolds in November 1991. He succeeded Albert Reynolds as leader of Fianna Fáil in November 1994. After the 1997 general election he entered coalition with the Progressive Democrats and was elected Taoiseach on 26th June 1997.

G ood Friday 1998 marked a truly historic moment in the pursuit of peace in Ireland. The Agreement concluded between all of the participating parties represents a major breakthrough in terms of consolidating peace and ending thirty years of conflict. For the first time an Agreement was created that was capable of winning strong support from both traditions in the North, from the people North and South, as well as enhancing co-operation throughout these islands. With the implementation of the full political settlement reached under the Good Friday Agreement, we have the strongest possible basis for permanent peace in Ireland, such an event has never been experienced in our history.

The Good Friday Agreement was the result of a long process of inclusive negotiations, for the first time involving representatives of all the traditions on this island; unionism, nationalism, loyalism and republicanism.

The context of the negotiations was set out at the beginning of the Agreement. In the Declaration of Support, all of the participants of the Agreement stated that they believed that there was a truly historic opportunity for a new beginning. The Declaration recognised that the tragedies of the past and their victims should never be forgotten, but could best be honoured through a fresh start dedicated to the achievement of reconciliation, tolerance, and mutual trust, and to the participation and vindication of the human rights of all. The participants committed themselves to partnership, equality and mutual respect as the basis of all the relationships within these islands. They further reaffirmed their commitment to non-violence and pledged to work to ensure the success of each and every one of the arrangements to be established.

The outcome of the negotiations, the Good Friday Agreement, addresses the key relationships on these islands, within Northern Ireland, between North and South and between Ireland and Britain, in addition to addressing the fundamental constitutional issues and all of the other issues of concern, human rights, reconciliation and the concerns of the victims of violence, economic, social and cultural issues, the decommissioning of paramilitary weapons, the normalisation of security arrangements, the future of policing and of the criminal justice system, and the release of prisoners.

The whole basis of the settlement is the recognition that we have to live together on this island, and for that we need peace, stability and reconciliation. The beliefs and opinions of both traditions must be respected and accommodated and neither can be allowed to impose its will on the other. To achieve such an accommodation involves, for everyone, changes in our ways of thinking, greater understanding and toleration and the will to build relationships across communities.

Taking all of these issues together and building one comprehensive framework provides a sound foundation on which peace can be fostered and relationships can be developed between individuals and between communities.

The principles of consent and cross-community support are central to the Good Friday Agreement. The institutions are designed to operate on a fair and cross-community basis, with all key decisions being taken on this basis. This means that the support of both traditions is required before action is taken in key areas, ensuring cross-community support for the work of the administration.

The Agreement provides for the protection of human rights to ensure that everyone is treated with respect and dignity as a human being. The central importance of equality, social, economic and cultural issues is acknowledged. Provisions have been made to recognise all identities and ensure equality, fairness and a voice for all.

The desire for a normal life, free from the pain and suffering experienced by both communities throughout the conflict, can be felt across Northern Ireland. To achieve this desire considerable change is needed. The Good Friday Agreement sets out to bring about that change. There now exists an opportunity to achieve change and to achieve a better, more peaceful future for everyone.

The benefits of a lasting peace for both traditions in Northern Ireland, and for all the people of these islands, are immeasurable. Providing a future where children can grow up without the constant threat of violence in their lives will be a truly great accomplishment. In an environment of peace, better understanding and relationships can be developed between communities, enhancing the quality of life of everyone.

The Good Friday Agreement provides for a new beginning. Work must continue to achieve the effective bedding down and implementation of the Agreement and, through that process, the delivery of tangible benefits to all elements of society in Northern Ireland and these islands, so that, through the necessary building of confidence, a lasting peace will be consolidated and maintained and a stable framework sustained, in which prosperity and reconciliation can flourish.

I believe that there is a strong desire on the part of all the parties to ensure that the promise of the Good Friday Agreement for the future of all people on this island is fully realised and that the major gains and achievements are preserved and built upon. I, and the Government I lead, are determined to work tirelessly to overcome all obstacles to the creation of a lasting peace in Ireland.

Forging Peace, Unlocking the Human Heart

Mary Bigley

Mary Bigley is a graduate of the University of Limerick and Dublin City University. She is a researcher and writer who also runs her own business in enabling organisations to develop their capacity, systems and policies. Originally from Athlone, she now lives in Dublin with her husband.

W e have not as yet succeeded in building a peaceful world. With whom does that responsibility lie? In whom does that capacity lie?

Much of what is written about the subject of peace building is written firstly with reference to the cessation and resolution of armed conflict and secondly with the emphasis on the political process. Much of what is written also considers peace to be that which prevails in the absence of war or armed conflict or the threat of armed conflict and it is upon such situations that the focus, energy, resources and commitment to building peace is concentrated. There is also a prevailing tendency to believe that the building of peace is the domain of politicians, international organisations and the institutions of the state and governance. Those of us who are fortunate enough to live in parts of the world which are not engaged in armed conflict tend also to look on at conflicts in the rest of the world as third party observers, lamenting and regretting the violence and the loss of life, but remaining somewhat untouched by it and seeing ourselves as outside of it.

It is, in my own view, these very ways of thinking which limit our ability to transform conflict and to create the kinds of communities and societies in which human beings may live in harmony and in which each human being may fulfil his or her unique potential. Seeing war as being the opposite of peace is fundamentally flawed – for this type of thinking permits us to allow the conditions for war to flourish unhindered within our societies – neglect of the human spirit, apathy, a desire for effortless, easily gained happiness and peace of mind, a deep reluctance to challenge ourselves and the numerous ways in which we limit ourselves.

Where there are human beings there is the potential for harmonious, dynamic, creative and loving relationships based on an unwavering and profound respect for life. Where there are human beings, there is the potential for tense, abusive, conflictual, violent and destructive relationships based on hatred, blame and profound disrespect. The responsibility and capacity to forge relationships which move along this continuum towards creation or towards destruction lies within the heart and mind of each and every human being. I am convinced that the transformation of our world is realised as each one of us takes on the challenge of actively transforming our own hearts and minds – developing and nurturing our humanity and, consequently, our relationships with human beings in our environment. I believe that the key to this sort of transformation lies in developing the greatest expression of our humanity – compassion.

Jihi – The Buddhist concept of compassion
Naturally, life is concerned with its preservation and human beings are concerned with their own self-preservation – instinctively, we avoid

10

situations of danger. Most of the human race would accept that the instinct for survival is innate – that it is part of the condition of being a human being.

Buddhism believes that the quality or attribute of compassion is also innate in human beings. The Japanese term for compassion is *jihi*. The character which signifies this concept is a rendition in Chinese characters of two ancient Indian terms – *maitri* – the giving of pleasure and karuna – the elimination of suffering. Deconstructing it in this manner would suggest that it is close in meaning to the Christian concept of 'love'. It is easy to find examples of the demonstration of this kind of compassion or love among those who are bound by familial or kinship ties. Parents have sacrificed or endangered their own lives to save those of their children – their actions frequently arise as instinctually as those which arise to preserve the self. Ties of this sort also are not the only motivation for such compassion – there are many who have endangered or lost their lives in the attempt to save the lives of perfect strangers. This notion of a universal compassion which one person is capable of extending to all humanity is captured by Argentinean author Hernandez when the gaucho hero, *Martin Fierro*, from the work of the same name declares:

> *"Happiness and unhappiness of all my brothers*
> *Are my own happiness and unhappiness.*
> *In their proud minds*
> *Will they bear my way of life.*
> *Forever will my passions*
> *Remember me always."*

11

These examples are obviously drawn from the extreme end of the continuum of action and it will only be in the minority of lives that situations will arise which may require compassionate actions of such magnitude. However, in the ordinary workaday world, there are countless examples of human compassion – actions taken by people to 'give pleasure to' and 'remove the suffering of' others. Buddhism conceives this compassion to be entirely natural and innate and believes it to arise as a result of an awareness of the inherent dignity of each and every life and the profound interconnectedness of all life.

This is not to say that it is equally well developed in all people – the desire to develop a particular quality or talent – followed up with the appropriate action will - in a very straightforward manner - result in the enhancement of that quality or attribute. Those who spend years developing their physical strength and fitness will clearly surpass in ability those who have invested little time or energy in doing so. A life of studying and reading exercises the brain and generally results in an ability to argue, debate and write more cogently and persuasively as the effort continues. A life spent learning how to hate and inflict pain produces highly effective torturers. A life spent fighting injustice develops courage and a life devoted to relieving the pain of others develops compassion.

The point of these examples is to demonstrate that all of these attributes are inherent in all human beings – those who seek to find the worst in humanity will see it and those who seek to find the best in human beings will see it – often simultaneously! Which of the two is right? Our judgements of other people is an entirely subjective matter – Zohar and Marshall's concepts of *'categories of thought'* here becomes instructive. According to our system of thought, we divide human beings into categories worthy of varying reactions and feelings – those we hate, love, tolerate or to whom we remain indifferent – what we see is a reflection of our own subjective feelings, which arise from our own particular *Weltanschauung.* In the example above, both are right – but rather more about their own subjective reality than humanity. A life based on *'categories of thought'* 'sees' a very different humanity than one based on compassion.

Ubuntu – An African concept of Humanity

> *"...there is a need for understanding but not for vengeance, a need for reparation but not for retaliation, a need for ubuntu but not for victimisation."* (Promotion of National Unity and Reconciliation Act No. 34 of 1995, South Africa).

Meaning 'humanity', *ubuntu* is related to two further African terms. *Umuntu* – *"the category of intelligent human force that includes spirits, the human dead and the living".* And *ntu* – *"God's being as metadynamic – active rather than metaphysical".* *Ubuntu,* therefore, implies an awareness of connectedness – a commonality shared between human beings – purely and simply because they are human beings. The transmission of this into a daily life philosophy, which guides how human beings should live, is conveyed through the Xhosa expression – *"ubuntu ungamntu ngabanye abantu"* which translates approximately as *"the expression of the humanity of a human being lies in relationships with other human beings"* or Shutte's translation – *"a person depends on other people to be a person".*

13

These concepts are not simply a body of esoteric thought, but a way of thinking which has application and function to daily life – they emphasise the active rather that the metaphysical, they constitute applied rather than theoretical philosophies. They take on their meaning in their application to the daily struggles of life and are, in this sense, distinguishable from dogma.

The Practical Application of Compassion

We begin the process of dehumanising ourselves and others from the moment we begin to perceive others as being some sort of collectivity, category, type or group – this way of seeing the world begins before we are even born and continues right throughout our lives. The nature of the category and the numbers of people embraced by it will vary, but the tendency towards seeing ourselves and those dear to us as individuals and others as part of one grouping or another is deeply embedded in our way of thinking.

The categorisation of any group of people is the beginning of the dehumanising process. From the moment we cease to perceive people as individuals but as a category of some sort is the moment from which we commence our journey towards 'them' and 'us' – 'my kind of people' and 'not my kind of people' – Muslims, men, women, Americans, Travellers, gays - the list of categories into which we place people to conform with our world view and make ourselves comfortable – refusing to go beyond the zone of comfort to which we have grown accustomed – is endless.

The problem with this way of perceiving others is that it permits us to dehumanise – to deny, withhold or trample all over the humanity and the human rights of all of the individuals who form part of that group. It equally contributes nothing to our understanding of our own and others humanity – it entirely clouds our vision, it influences every interaction we have with members of that group in a way that allows us to further confirm that indeed we are right about them, it leaves injustices and inequalities firmly in place and allows the seeds of hatred to flourish.

The building of an interdependent community is made possible and indeed is entirely natural in a life based on compassion for I now know that my humanity is bound up in recognising your humanity, in dehumanising you, I dehumanise myself – human beings are made for togetherness.

This in no way discounts the individual at the expense of the community – while human beings are created for togetherness – each individual remains unique and distinctive – the potential inherent in each human life uniquely develops in the midst of unified diversity. Conflict arises not because human beings exhibit their distinctiveness or uniqueness, but because many aim to exhibit their superiority.

This way of thinking humanises the 'other', the 'enemy' or the 'oppressor' because their humanity is inextricably bound up with ours as ours is bound up in theirs. This way of living implies more than the creation of a society in which the humanity of each is the defining factor. It is the point to which we might continually return to check for ourselves the quality of our own communities – regardless of whether these be families, workplaces, housing estates or countries. We might make it not only the cornerstone of our future communities, but also the building block of the process whereby we struggle towards the creation of such communities. Such a way of thinking has tremendous transformative power, it transcends boundaries. It defines people not according to sets of characteristics conferred on them by their ethnic background, gender, language or other attributes, but by the relationships between them and others.

Defining what it is we mean by peace and working towards its achievement is the business of each and every human being. Each and every human being has a role to play within their own families, communities and workplaces – each one that plays their part to the fullest makes a contribution, while the contribution of those who do not is sorely missed.

> *"Peace is an intangible value, a cultural state of soul and mind that must be so clear and strong within each individual and so widely shared as a vital necessity by other people that it becomes the common patrimony of society at large. Peace will thus come to exist only when all, or a great majority of, the citizens come to treasure it as something precious and worth committing themselves to. Whereas war is the distilled gall of arrogance, egoism, mutual distrust and fear and is almost invariably brewed up by the wielders of power, peace is the natural outcome of mutual comprehension, tolerance, respect and solidarity among people and can spring only from the heart of the people themselves"* (Pecci & Ikeda, 1984).

Confident Communities

May Blood

Baroness Blood is a founder member of the Northern Ireland Women's Coalition and was a member of the Coalition talks team for the duration of the multi-party peace talks, which culminated in the Good Friday Agreement. Throughout her working life, she has been an advocate for those living with the effects of poverty. A former cutter in a mill, she has been a full-time community worker since 1990. She was made a life peer in 1999 for her services to community work.

I spent some time dwelling on what would be the best way to approach the subject of peace. I came to the conclusion that because of where I am in the Shankill, here in the midst of a Protestant community, it is how the peace process is viewed by that community at this moment in time that is important to the future of peace in Northern Ireland. In view of the fact that we have recently had very serious internal rioting many people on the ground have said, "the IRA has stopped shooting us, but now the loyalist paramilitaries will shoot each other and where is the peace in that?"

For many people in this area it is difficult to see the benefits of peace. I travel all over Northern Ireland, so I see the products of peace, but many people who never leave this area are asking questions, and I think that is where Mr. Trimble is coming in for his hardest criticism. Because in Protestant communities like the Shankill they are not actually seeing the positive aspects of the peace process.

Elections in this area demonstrate this feeling as people move away from support of mainstream parties and weigh in behind those that would be considered to be parties on the periphery. For many years here in the community, elections in this area would have been characterised by people 'following the flag'. But I find more and more people are giving some constructive thought to who they might want. I think it is only at its initial stages but, if that grows within the Protestant community, you could see a withdrawal of support for the Democratic Unionist Party (DUP), but you could also see reluctance to support the Ulster Unionist Party (UUP). One of the things that greatly heartened people in the Shankill area was the upsurges of the Progressive Unionist Party (PUP) and the Ulster Democratic Party (UDP), they look like Unionist parties who were looking after bread and butter issues.

Now a majority of people in my area would view the Ulster Unionists as the fur coat brigade. That is actually their nickname. Many in the area believe they support the middle class and they do not really look after working class issues. Areas that suffer the depravation like we have in the Shankill seem to have been skimmed over. On the other end of it, you have the DUP who wave the flag and you must follow that flag at all costs. Many people would cling to that idea because there is a certainty about it. The DUP has never changed their record in thirty years, it has always been known. However, support for the DUP is like always having an illness where the doctor is continually giving you tablets that cannot cure it, but simply relieve it temporarily. Many people in the Protestant community find themselves in this situation and are starting to look for alternatives.

It is an entirely different day for the Catholic community. There is a great resurgence in the Catholic community and a great confidence about them. Both their political wings, the Social Democratic and Labour Party (SDLP) and Sinn Féin, have emerged as very confident and looking towards the future. I think Protestants feel a little left out of the process for that reason. On one hand we have Mr. Trimble telling us that the future can be bright; on the other hand we have Mr. Paisley telling us the future will be dark. I remember speaking in Catholic West Belfast one night and said for Catholics it is relatively easy, there is only one enemy, the British. For Protestants it is extremely difficult because we have a bogeyman behind every door.

I heard a leading Protestant saying that Belfast will become a Catholic city, and that is the great fear of the Protestants who live in Belfast. There is, particularly here in the Shankill, the feeling of alienation. Many Protestants have up and moved out to the periphery. You find them in places like North Down which is predominantly Protestant. The fact is that on both sides of the Shankill we have a large Catholic communty and we are getting no real clear real leadership in the middle. There is that feeling that we have been circled around and we are here, here to stay, and that gives people a very negative outlook. However, in the work we have been trying to do here in the Greater Shankill Partnership, we have been trying to ask people to look to the future, to the next ten or fifteen years. It is extremely difficult when people are very apathetic about where they are going politically.

The Good Friday Agreement was signed and here on the road there was euphoria over that, people here accepted it and thought it was great. The euphoria present during the early days of the Agreement reaffirms the understanding that people in Northern Ireland want peace. However to say that they would like peace for the sake of peace would be to mis-state their position. Peaceful settlement in Northern Ireland depends on both sides feeling comfortable with the way in which peace is achieved. The best way to achieve this is for the communities to construct peace, that is to say, to build peace from the ground up.

It is important for the Protestant community to become more confident in itself. I would hope that a belief would develop in the Greater Shankill area, and indeed in the whole Protestant community in Northern Ireland, that they can take part in whatever the future holds and firmly establish our role in that future. This should not be through any sense of 'taking over', but instead through a genuine desire to work together. The most important factor which is lacking in the Protestant community at the moment is a confidence in the future, and a preparedness to play a full part in it.

As far as the Peace Process is concerned, you cannot put the Genie back in the bottle. Peace, and the idea of a peaceful settlement, is a fact of life. You see it in any number of things, for instance even the politicians language has changed. Terms such as 'negotiate' are as much a part of the political language today as 'scorched earth' was a few years back. I think that from a Protestant viewpoint, the notion that there will eventually be peace in Northern Ireland is inevitable, however, that does not mean that the communities will open up to any kind of peace. For peace to work, it cannot be imposed from the top down. It must be an agreed solution where both communities do not feel threatened. For the peace process to be successful it must come from the bottom up. Peace is dependent upon the resolution of the internal problems in the Protestant community, but those problems are something for the community to solve, not the politicians.

Beneath the rule of men entirely great,
the pen is mightier than the sword.

Edward Bulwer-Lytton

Tribal Warfare

Jack Bourke

*Councillor Jack Bourke served three terms as Fianna Fáil Mayor of
Limerick. He is the Chairman of the Mid-Western Health Board and
the Limerick Institute of Technology.*

When invited to make a literary contribution to *Pens for Peace*, a basic
rule of science came to mind, cause and effect. The cause is
inevitably domination. The effect, invariably, mans inhumanity to man.

A brief scan at world history.

The Roman Empire: they dominated every tribe in central and western
Europe, including England, Scotland and Wales - for some obscure reason
they ignored Ireland.

The Ottoman Empire: Turkey, Iran, Russia, Egypt, Africa - the same old
story, they over-ran and subjugated any tribe whose path they crossed.

The British Empire: too vast to list out here; suffice to mention there are
seventy-seven countries in the British Commonwealth of Nations.

The Soviet Union; Russia, Armenia, Azerbaijan, Belorussia, Estonia,
Georgia, Kazakhstan, Kirghiza, Latvia, Lithuania, Moldavia, Tadzhikistan,
Turkmenistan, Ukraine, Uzbekistan not any more, the tribes revolted.

Yugoslavia: Bosnia, Hercegovina, Croatia, Macedonia, Serbia, Slovenia, Kosovo, Vojvodina - Tito managed to keep the tribes under control until he went to his 'reward', then all hell broke loose.

The Hundred Years War between England and France: fought over England's claim by Edward III to the Throne of France. Ah! The glory of it all.

The Seven Years War 1756-1763 by Britain and Prussia against France, Austria and Russia: they fought for the control of Germany, North America, India and more tribes than I can enumerate here.

The history of the Jews from the Twelve Hebrew Tribes to the present day when the conflict between the Israelites and the Palestinians is unceasing - in one moment they talk about peace, at the same time they slaughter each other; this one will run and run.

Afghans, how could I leave them out. They consist of many different tribes, the Pathans - the only true Afghans, Durani, Chilzais, Tajiks from Iran, Uzbeks and Hazaras. Afghanistan is very much in the news right now because they are slaughtering each other and millions of their people are in refugee camps on the borders of Pakistan and Iran where they have fled from persecution.

The Afghans are also providing shelter and a base for the evil Bin Laden who is misusing history as a terrorist weapon. He will never be forgotten or forgiven for September 11th, 2001.

I have gone through the exercise in this way merely to illustrate that tribes can be conquered, their lands and possessions usurped, they can be kept under control for 'a time' but eventually the tribes will revolt and demand their freedom and the right to chart their own destiny.

While I have no wish to portray the six north eastern Counties of the Province of Ulster in a league with the aforementioned, the inescapable fact is that since 'the Flight of the Earls' and the vast plantation of Ulster in the seventeenth century, the Province is now populated by two tribes, the Loyalist-Planters - wealthy, powerful and dominant and the Natives - now subjugated. To this day the Loyalists are the ascendant class, albeit a bitterly divided group-community. Both tribes have paramilitary organisations. The paramilitaries on the Nationalist side have declared a ceasefire and destroyed some of their armoury and please God they will soon completely destroy whatever remains. Hopefully, the paramilitaries of the other tribe will do likewise.

Ulster is a very beautiful province and the vast majority of it's population are fine and generous people. In sport we have teams representing all of the island of Ireland. It begs the question, why, in the twenty-first century, can't the two tribes of Ulster co-exist, work as a team, and live in peace and harmony?

The day of peace and tranquillity I believe will come, as long as men and women of vision continue with dialogue and compromise.

I suppose the same formula could be used to cure all the ills that exist on planet Earth.

Cultural Fusion

sculpture of a hurler and rugby player in Limerick

An Equitable Peace
James Buttimer

James Buttimer received a Master of Arts Degree in History from Armstrong Atlantic State University in Savannah, Georgia. He worked for twenty years in the construction industry before returning to school in 1994. He is active in the Ancient Order of Hibernians and the current Chairman of the Savannah Irish Festival. Along with his wife and daughter, he hosted children associated with the Children's Friendship Project of Northern Ireland and recently helped write and produce the documentary 'Georgia's Sisters of Mercy'.

The pursuit of peace is of necessity defined by the conflict it attempts to resolve. The conflict is often bitter, vicious, and passed from one generation to the next until it assumes an aura of inevitability that is inescapable. The initial goal of peacemakers is to break the psyche of inertia and fatalism surrounding apparently intractable conflicts to permit the flourishing of the new possibilities and hope that peace may bring. In this sense peace is not simply the absence of conflict, but rather a better vision of the future in which the hopes and aspirations of all parties involved in the conflict may be addressed as fully as possible. To wrest these hard-won goals from the cycle of conflict, the peace process is best served by those who can articulate the better vision of the future while implementing the difficult political and cultural necessities requisite to a peace process. In short, trust is won by addressing the fears of the opposing faction.

A just compromise forms the heart of the most enduring peace initiatives. A comprehensive peace will also address issues of social justice and equal protection under the rule of law. For this to have the greatest impact it is necessary for each side to be able to acknowledge the value of what the other offers as well as the fears imbedded in historical conflict. Crucial to this end are negotiators of goodwill possessing the ability to view the conflict from the opposing side. Specifically, one must acknowledge the individual human suffering caused by the conflict.

Perhaps the most difficult aspect of a peace process is the incremental nature of success beginning with the laborious confidence-building measures necessary for dialogue to begin that will ultimately yield the fruit of the better vision of the future. Patience and constancy are the hallmark virtues required, but these can only be brought to bear effectively in a general absence of violence and provocation. Once extremists are allowed to hijack the peace process by the resumption of atrocities, the role of the peacemaker is greatly diminished. Those who would counsel patience in the face of murder are most often consigned to a pathetic irrelevancy in the eyes of the greater community. The difficulty of course is devising ways for the greater community to take the initiative away from extremists and set the agenda for peacemaking.

From my own experience of the civil rights struggle in America, it seems crucial to create opportunities for the many people of goodwill on opposing sides of a conflict to voice their demands for an end to conflict and to seek reconciliation on the common ground of our humanity. Too often political and cultural leaders have a vested interest in keeping the pot boiling over some perceived grievance to their ideology or social supremacy. The resultant cynicism and despair silence those who would give peace a chance and alienate many more from politics. However, if the frustration of this large but despairing mass of people can be given voice and action, it may be just the thing to give a politician or leader the courage to table the rant of ideology and demagoguery. More importantly, it would put into perspective the destructive and violent objections of extremists. Eventually political institutions must give the peace process time to grow the legs necessary to mature and affect generational change.

All the pieces appear to be in place for peace to take hold in Northern Ireland. It is obvious that many people have thought deeply about the need to wrench the society out of the vicious cycle of historical violence. Both visionaries and realists have had their say, and importantly, the people of goodwill on all sides have made their voices heard in the cause of lasting peace. Unfortunately, the politicians have been less than creative in advancing the peace process to the stability it demands and confronting those who throw obstacles in the way of the ultimate goal - a just and equitable society respecting all traditions. Most disturbing is the reluctance of political leaders to spend the political capital gained by advancing the peace process rather than horde it. The Unionist leadership should be ashamed of the lack of leadership demonstrated. Some things are worth risking political careers on, yet they cautiously allowed the obstructionists, who will raise one objection after another, to rule their actions instead of boldly advancing the better vision of the future. Sinn Féin mistakenly address every issue as if it is speaking only to the British government and hostile loyalists, while failing to recognise it is playing to a much bigger audience on a grander stage now. Why have they not been able to move past their tired ideology and the objections of their most obstinate members to address those persons of goodwill in the broader population? A little political savvy would have gone a long way in defusing the whole disarmament demand. A token disarmament would have pressured those who claim to be so concerned about the issue, to put up or shut up. The civil rights of blacks in America were won only after the federal government made clear that it was willing to risk confrontation with white supremacist in order to affect change. The British government seems incapable of confronting hard-liners, either in its own security system or in Northern Ireland, in spite of the overwhelming desire of the people in Britain and Northern Ireland to do so. What a shame if the politicians fail to deliver the peace so longed for by their people. Old ways die hard, but peace, when it gains a foothold, can prove to be a tenacious advocate in its own right.

Shannon's Peace

Martin Byrnes

Martin Byrnes is the Deputy Editor of the Limerick Leader.

M uch of what I write here relates in some way to Shannon. To begin with, I recall traveling in a special train from Limerick to Drogheda and sharing a compartment with a man of legend. It was late 1976 and we were each traveling to become a small part of the massive peace march at the new Peace bridge over the symbolic Boyne. That winter's day we prayed in the chilly fog, and Joan Baez sang, and I shared a compartment on the way home with the same man, Dr. Brendan O'Regan. I didn't speak. I listened. I had not known then that he was founder of the fledgling Southern Movement for Peace, a solidarity group in sympathy with the Peace People in Northern Ireland, or that it would grow to become Co-operation North, later Co-operation Ireland, or that that would facilitate the creation of the Irish Peace Institute at the University of Limerick.

I had known that Brendan O'Regan had begun his celebrated public career in the shadow of conflict as Manager of the State's catering and accommodation organisation at the flying boat base at Foynes, and that he had held that position for almost exactly the duration of the Second World War. In those times, Irish neutrality at Foynes was little more than pretence. Those seaplanes which kept communications open between Southampton and New York La Guardia, refuelling at Foynes in Ireland and Botwood in Newfoundland, were exclusively Allied machines, even if

31

they were painted in civil livery. Most of the planes had been purchased by, and leased back from, the US Government to minimise cash losses to airlines in the event of any being shot down. Foynes turned an unofficial blind eye; after all, no armaments or the like were being airlifted. Yet, it can be said that those transatlantic contacts contributed in a quantifiable way towards keeping official America informed prior to her entering the European theatre, and perhaps thereby to the earlier restoration of peace in Europe.

And when hostilities were finally over, it was principally Shannon, inaugurated on the Clare shore in 1945, which held the door open for the rejuvenation of Europe and the increased economic cohesion between the two northern continents. And Brendan O'Regan was the man in charge of the development of Shannon in all its facets for three further decades.

Let's look at a somewhat different Shannon connection: until 1994, all flights from North America to Dublin had to stop at Shannon in each direction. In that year a decade-long rearguard action to defend the *status quo* was lost. However, because of a continuing upturn in transatlantic traffic as the after-effects of the Gulf War on willingness to fly abated, both Dublin and Shannon found themselves with profitable direct flights to JFK.

But this left Aer Lingus with a wide-bodied intercontinental aeroplane parked for wasteful hours on the Rineanna tarmac. So it was decided to market that time, and the plane was sent on to Manchester, and Aer Lingus tried to sell Manchester-Kennedy flights with a short stopover in Shannon.

But, due to competition, that didn't work too well. Then someone noticed that Northern Ireland had no direct connection to the USA – to JFK in particular. And a little research determined that Belfast businesspeople wouldn't mind a half-hour stopover at Shannon, not least because EU citizens would continue to enjoy the benefit of Shannon's famous duty-free shopping on the outbound leg. As a result, now, nobody in the Mid West would dream of driving to Northern Ireland while flights 112/111 get us there and back in silken comfort, and considerable contacts between the north-eastern and south-western quadrants of the island have been established and constantly improved. To this day, the swish A330 connection between Belfast International at Aldergrove and JFK, via Shannon, is a tangible contribution toward understanding between people, a conduit for investment and a valuable link between industry and academe.

Another Shannon of course is the river itself and the Shannon-Erne waterway, now re-opened along its whole length, performs the same Ulster-Munster linkage, albeit in a far more sedate, if equally comfortable, way. An engineering problem remains in the new constant-head weir in the middle of Limerick city, but that should be solved sooner rather than later. Shortly, it should be as commonplace to cruise from Kilrush as far as Belleek for leisure as it is to fly from Shannon to Aldergrove on business.

Let me conclude by reaffirming that work toward peace and understanding indeed revolves around Shannon - but also around Garryowen, Young Munsters and UL Bohemians...

The popular, almost proletarian democracy which is Limerick rugby, especially in the city, but increasingly in the towns and parishes, comes as a pleasant shock to visiting Northern Ireland teams and supporters in the course of the AIB League season. This is the more so because Ulster rugby has yet to dispel even its own self-perception of being mainly of Protestant and Unionist tradition – and very much at the upper end at that. The existence of the AIB League created, for the first time, direct playing contacts between the clubs of the four provinces. The distances may be inconvenient at times, but the idea has worked.

When Ulster teams visit Limerick, the simple courtesy and breadth of sporting knowledge of 'non-blazers', displayed with clarity in discussions, which instinctively preclude any mention of politics, have been eye-openers to visitor after visitor. And this goodwill is redoubled by the expectation and promise of an equally open, warm and down to earth reception when Limerick travels north in reciprocation.

Much has been done, much more in fact than most people realise. Continued economic and social contacts, at a variety of levels, are reducing misunderstandings. It will take much patience, but then the Shannon has been flowing for a very long time.

A Perpetual Peace?
Matt Cannon

Matt Cannon received a Bachelor of Arts in International Relations/Political Science from Syracuse University in 1994. He completed his Ph.D. on the role of local governments in cross border co-operation at the University of Limerick in 2001. He works as the project/fundraising officer for the Irish Peace Institute.

P eace is a simple word, but a complex concept. Peace requires the absence of war. Yet, when the nature of war has changed, and when the presence of terrorism results in a constant war, how can peace be achieved? Peace is desirable, however, peace is not achieved through submission to tyranny. Terrorism, a word that has become extremely prevalent recently, is tyranny. As an American, it was not until the 11th of September that I confronted terrorism and the prospect of the ongoing threat of war. America had moved from a place where peace was always found internally and war was fought on distant shores to a paranoid nation that was afraid to board a plane or open the mail. Yes, I studied terrorism and worked in places whose aim was to alleviate the effects of it, however I never understood it. Never understood the sense of fear, alienation and shock associated with an act designed to intimidate.

In many senses terrorism is a war in slow motion. Terrorism cannot be distilled from civilised society as war once was. The very nature of war has changed so that civilian, non-combatant victims are the inevitable conclusion of the evolution of war. War was once characterised as a state of armed conflict between nation-states. In this type of conflict battles were fought and soldiers lost lives, however the civilian remained removed from conflict. The twentieth century witnessed an escalation of conflict and the change in the nature of war. War evolved into an increasingly brutal struggle where civilians were no longer considered separate from the conflict, but instead were deemed cogs in the war machine. This was validated by Hiroshima and Nagasaki where the distinction between combatant and non-combatant disappeared.

Terrorism has taken conflict to the next level. The response to terrorism, the *War on Terrorism*, seems to be trapped in twentieth century, or perhaps even nineteenth century, approaches to conflict. Attempts to defeat terrorism through the bombing of Afghanistan may eventually defeat one foe, however the pictures of bombed hospitals and injured civilians will only create more enemies. Admittedly, military efforts have not been the only instrument in the *War on Terrorism*, but they have been the most prominent one. To many the bombing of Afghanistan demonstrates the futility of using military means to defeat a threat that transgresses all aspects of civilised society. The belief that terrorism can be defeated by a military campaign carried out by a coalition of nation-states against rogue nation-states, demonstrates a fundamental misunderstanding of the nature of terrorism. Terrorism is transnational and feeds off the inability of sovereign nation-states to monitor their cross-border networks. The nation-state is a blunt tool, poorly equipped to fight a long-term war against terrorism.

Of course, those who have been victimised by terrorism have a natural initial reaction to suppress the supporters of terrorism. By criminalizing terrorism you strike out at potential threats to peace and security.

However, the history of terrorism demonstrates that simply defining terrorism as a criminal act does little to prevent it. In order to understand terrorism, America must look elsewhere, to places that have experienced and lived with terror. They must take note and learn the lessons that have been paid for with the lives of the victims of ongoing conflict. Northern Ireland witnessed horrific acts of inhumanity, acts that acted as a barrier, dividing communities and preventing understanding. Yet in the midst of this division and terror, some brave proponents of peace have found a way to construct a framework for reconciliation.

This framework was not constructed by top down elimination of the proponents of terror, but instead was forged through a gradual process of building trust from the bottom-up. Instead of continually fighting the symptoms of terror, the process of building relationships that cross borders and communities is essential to addressing misconceptions that feed terror. It is only through contact that you can change the minds of those who feel they are locked in a zero-sum game where the fear and alienation they feel result in support for terrorism to preserve a way of life.

Peace grows from the bottom-up. Peace must be constructed by the people and not imposed upon them. Imposing peace may work in the short-term, however the long-term consequences can be worse than the initial conflict. We need only look as far as the Balkans for an example of this. Tito was successful in containing one of the world's most infamous ethnic conflicts through fear and intimidation, however that solution was only temporary. The chaos we witness today in the Balkans is a testament to the need for peace from the bottom-up. Is this a call to end military and legal enforcement against terrorism? No, short-term prevention of terrorism requires a degree of enforcement and the deterrence of extremist groups that are willing to perpetuate violence for the sake of violence. However, those groups gain strength from populations that feel wronged or a desire to be heard. The only way to defeat terrorism in the long term and ensure a lasting peace is to address the misconceptions of the populations that have genuine grievances. The best way to approach this is through authentic attempts at promoting contact and exchange across borders.

The United States is only now coming to grips with the horrors of terrorism and the feelings of alienation, fear and shock associated with it. If we are to defeat terrorism in the next century, we need to move beyond the mind-set of the nation-state. Terrorism will not be defeated and peace will not be achieved through traditional military conflict between nation states. Efforts at using methods such as coalition building and international law enforcement networks are laudable, however they still fall short of the goal of providing long-term security. A 'perpetual peace' where justice exists internationally, where terrorism can be targeted specifically and where peace is the goal of every nation requires a bottom-up effort. I believe that in addition to enforcement strategies a new priority should be placed on promoting understanding between the West and Arab nations so that fundamentalist terrorists no longer find support from the moderate members of society. The best and only way to do this is to build peace from the bottom-up.

A Pluralist's Peace

Kate Casey

Kate Casey graduated with an MA in mathematics and an H.Dip.Ed. She travelled widely and worked in various jobs. For twenty years she was a lecturer in mathematics, now retired she is interested in philosophy, religion and politics.

The divide on this island is a cultural divide and the paramilitaries see themselves as cultural warriors. More contacts and greater competency in cross-culture communications will produce culture convergence and prevent culture conflict by exposing misrepresentation and stereotyping. An open society accommodates diversity in a living space where pluralist people make room for each other. There is room for the rat-tat of the lambeg drum, but not the tat-tat of the machine gun. A salad bowl provides diversity and a mixed diet is good for the body and mind. Culture enrichment comes from the interface of cultures in a melting pot, like cosmopolitan communities of large cities. A university is a creative community because it is universal in cultures and faculties and this helps us to change and grow. We grow by selling what is good in our culture and buying what is good in other cultures. The melting pots of the world are the creative spots of the world. A nation is not an imagined community but the same people living in the same place for a long time and if they want to cleave apart or coalesce with their neighbours; it is decided by referendum. All modern nations are the combination and integration of different peoples over the centuries. In an open society the politics of inclusion is stronger than the politics of illusion. The idea of a pure race is a foolish fantasy for fanatics as there has always been an ethnic mix and no pure culture has ever passed down unsullied by external influence. Tradition should inspire but not limit the vision. The white in our flag symbolises the melting pot. It requires us to combine and celebrate the green and orange. St. Patrick Day is green boosterism; the real meaning, the coming of Christianity, is a shared idealism. The Twelfth is orange but it too was a step forward for democracy as Constitutional Monarchy is better than Absolute Monarchy. Remembrance Sunday is about our role as British; these islands and the Commonwealth acting collectively to defend democracy. For peace and prosperity we need multi-national co-operation and integration and these relationships result in a more pluralist people. To avoid ghettos and the need for partition, people must learn to share common space with those who are different. Pluralist people should use the hyphen more often; Irish-British-European, just as Irish-American is used. Inclusiveness in remembrance and celebration will give us more carnivals and less carnage in the street. The Twelfth, like St. Patrick's Day, should be celebrated all over Ireland.

When righteousness flows like a stream, it refreshes social and economic life and peace flourishes. A righteous person has a set of values but also the skill to examine all values as to their true or false basis; this allows righteousness to grow. There are no borders between righteous people as love and rights are universal. A bill of rights enacted and obeyed will protect people's rights. Freedom is not government in a particular place, but a constitution that delivers democratic and human rights. Citizenship is a legal definition not based on race and everyone born there has the right to live there and celebrate his or her own particular culture.

Education should be hard on war and the causes of war. A developmental education in a creative community helps peace by growing 'tall' individuals. Tall individuals are more important than tall memorials. People's minds should be opened to the benefits of a free market in goods and ideas. Open markets and open minds have destroyed communism by the innovation of better products and methods of production. The human mind is like a parachute; opened it floats on high, closed it hits the ground. Civilisation is due to a master culture and not a master race. Heroes should be high achievers in any field; business, sport, academia, art etc.. A meritocracy is where the pecking order is based on a broad range of contributions in the workplace or community. Politicians who obey the will of the people should be acclaimed rather than glamorising men of violence for imposing their will on the people. Peace and prosperity are correlated with fertile brains; fighting and famine with fanatic brains.

> *"Could the spend on deadly weapons of terror,*
> *Go instead to redeem the human mind from error,*
> *Then wisdom and love will undo the pride of race,*
> *And build the New Jerusalem in this*
> *green and pleasant place."*

Louis Pasteur was anti-war and pro-prosperity. He wrote

> *"two opposing laws seem to me to be in contest - the one of a law of blood and death, forcing the nations always ready for battle; the other the relief of mankind. The one places a single life above all victories; the other sacrifices millions of lives to the ambition of a single individual. Which law will prevail God only knows, but of this we maybe sure - that science will obey the law of humanity and will always labour to enlarge the frontiers of life."*

We can now appreciate that the knowledge-based society has brought us better health and a better quality of life. To have a future individually we must act collectively. This is now more likely to happen as instant communication has turned the world into a global village. The people who want to push back the frontiers of knowledge are a blessing to mankind and those who want to push back the frontiers of their territory are a curse. Knowledge is an infinitely perfectible product and only large economic units can afford the intellectual capital and financial capital to keep pace in the technology race. Keeping pace requires about a half million workers in research and this means a unit of two hundred million people at least is necessary. Economic forces will erode borders and the values that will integrate and unite people in large units are also the values that will use technology wisely. Such values are enlightened self-interest and mutual co-operation to create more wealth, to seek a fair division and that if there are any losers, they are duly compensated. Nationalism promotes selfishness that seeks gains and not count the costs inflicted on their neighbours. Such nationalism leads to trade wars and real wars. To economists, nationalism is a sewer down which flowed the blood and wealth of Europe. Nationalist wars turned mountains of gold into lakes of blood.

All militarism is a threat to peace. Prussian culture caused two world wars. By militarism I mean where the military control or have undue influence on the government. Germany was united by the gun and what is united by force must be ruled by force. Kaiser Germany was an example where the Kaiser made Germany great but the German people small. The people were mere slaves of a vicious military machine. The golden thread of civilisation is the strict civilian control of the military. In World War One, a military Junta of the Kaiser and two Generals controlled Germany.

The army and state in close embrace, Sitting upon a servile German race.

The economy, education and social life was run for the benefit of the military. The values of patriotism, discipline and heroism were fostered. Einstein saw this at first hand in Germany and wrote;

"he who joyfully marches to music in rank and file has already earned my contempt. He has been given a large brain by mistake, since for him the spinal cord could suffice. This disgrace to humanity should be done away with at once. Heroism at command, senseless brutality, deplorable love of country stance, how I despise it. How despicable and ignoble war is."

The talents of military men are necessary to defend the realm and protect the person. The right to life means the state must protect us from illegal violence by using minimum force. Because of this the state maintains a security force and we owe a debt of gratitude to the army and police who risk their lives to protect us. Only the state is allowed to maintain an army and no political party must have a private army or it could act like the Nazi party in Germany, take over the state and destroy democracy. Our constitution wisely has a provision (article 15-6-2) that no organization, except the state, can raise and maintain an army for any purpose whatsoever. The talents of the military mind are not the talents to make a good politician where powers of persuasion are necessary. A military man operates in a pyramid power that sits on the people. A politician mobilises people power to get things done; but the people sit on him.

Ecumenism in religion is important for peace. We are all made in God's image; that is our invisible part and we differ only in the less important outer part. The religious divide in Ireland gives the fault lines. The metal barriers are correlated with the mental barriers. Christianity should foster universal brotherhood;

> *"Father may they be in us, just as you are in me as I am in you. May they be one, so that the world will believe that you sent me. I in them and you in me, so that they may be completely one."* (John 17-23)

Christianity should break down barriers by shared worship and shared idealism as in the revealed religion of the Bible. A mixed education would unite and benefit students from a diversity of the knowledge of God. Unity does not have to mean uniformity. The truth, as developed by congregational power as well as pyramid power, will add to our understanding. Sectarianism means people have enough religion to be arrogant but not enough to be humble and see the invisible spark of God in everyone. Dogma divides and some people will kill for dogma rather than grow in knowledge from debate and the synergy of mixed perceptions. We are human and all human knowledge is imperfect and all knowledge, even scientific knowledge, is evolving so absolutism is dangerous as it assumes perfect knowledge. Still, not to be deterred, we can grow in wisdom and in seeking and gaining wisdom we are seeing an improved reflection of God and His celestial wisdom. The Bible tells us not to boast of our strength or wealth but we can boast of our knowledge of God. The Bible also requests us to make the world as full of the knowledge of God as the seas are of water.

Once there were two holy men from a people who were divided by religion and sometimes differed violently. The two holy men went up a mountain to live and pray in a cave. They prayed that God would bring the law and the necessary grace to unite the people. After much prayer God appeared as a bright light and told them that there were only two main commandments to love God and to love man. The people were to assemble outside the cave one week from that day and He would appear in the cave, but the people were to look in the other direction, as the bright light would blind them. He would bring them the law and the grace. The holy men told the people the news but the people wanted to see God. They went to the scientists and the scientists said they would make a prism to cover the mouth of the cave and it would refract the white light and the people could safely look. God appeared and the people could see as the prism refracted the white light into different colours. God told them there were only two laws to love Him and their fellow man. If they did this He would fill them with grace and joy. This duly happened and the people mixed, danced and hugged each other. But as the groups mixed, some said God was a lovely blue colour, others that He was a green colour and still others said He was a red colour. A dispute broke out and became acrimonious and the divide became so bad that the scientists could not get them to understand that they were all seeing white light but the prism bent it into different colours; so that standing at different locations they had different perspectives. Peace comes from being able to add the different perspectives together to see the bright white light. We are all called to be peacemakers and not nationalists. We are called to reconcile not to divide, to mix so that our hearts, like the waters of the river Shannon that comes from many different sources, may be mingled in peace.

It is when you give of yourself that you truly give.

Kahlil Gibran

Dialogue Workshops:
Enabling protagonists to build new relationships of understanding
Geoffrey Corry

Geoffrey Corry BA(Mod) MSc(Mgmt) HDipEd is a management consultant specialising in conflict resolution and mediation in the workplace, community, the environment and family settings. He is currently chair of the Mediators Institute Ireland. He is the Facilitator for the political dialogue workshops held at the Glencree Centre for Reconciliation and Programme Director of the Glencree Summer School. He visited South Africa for two months (1985) with a bursary from the Christian Fellowship Trust and Israel/Palestine for two weeks (1998) as part of an EU delegation. He also worked as course director for the UCD adult education modules on conflict resolution and visiting lecturer in mediation at the Irish School of Ecumenics and the UCD Diploma in Mediation Studies.

B ack in the late 70's, when the outlook was rather gloomy in the peace movement in Ireland, some of us were kept going by our elusive search for the real meaning of the concept of reconciliation. I was involved with the Glencree Centre for Reconciliation up in the Wicklow hills and we had done lots of different things - seminars on weighty political themes of federalism and new models of political co-operation, exchange trips between north and south in Ireland and walks of remembrances in Dublin for our own unhealed civil war split.

But it was the visit by Dr Adam Curle (a wise Quaker, veteran mediator and first head of Bradford University Peace Studies) to Glencree in 1981 that switched on a new light for me. He said ever so quietly that "reconciliation involved the building of a new relationship of understanding through an act of love, compassion or restitution". What was different about Curle's definition was its emphasis on process - the relational journey that each must make toward the other so as to connect with the pain of their past suffering and their sense of historic grievance. Up to then I was probably caught up in the moral and churchy imperative that "you must forgive" and be reconciled to your brother and sister, without grasping the amount of re-perception and changed attitude that is necessary to underpin any new way forward.

Intergroup interaction

My visit to South Africa in 1985 at a time of great turmoil in their struggle with the injustice of apartheid, brought me in contact with Hendrik van der Merwe of the Centre for Intergroup Studies in Cape Town. He introduced me to new thinking about mediation and some of the emerging negotiation and conflict resolution theory in the USA. In 1987 I underwent mediation training in San Francisco with the help of Ray Shonholtz of Community Boards and suddenly I realised that the only way we have a chance of protagonists coming to "a new relationship of understanding" with each other is through an interactive, intergroup communication experience that is facilitated by a third party.

It must be interactive because new relational understandings will come out of face-to-face engagement with each other - starting out with hearing each other's painful experience of past suffering and going all the way to connecting with the underlying source of the other's alienation. This level of experiential engagement and grounding in the other's perceived realities simply does not happen in proximity talks or shuttle mediation efforts where the parties are separated into different rooms.

In protracted ethnic conflict situations, it must also be intergroup because the process involves more than an interpersonal experience between two people. Each person participating in a conflict resolution workshop is coming in some form of representative capacity on behalf of their party and with the knowledge of their leadership. It works best if they are in a sub-leadership role within their party or in a back-up professional support role so that they can report back into the party.

By the early 1990's, I was ready to try out this different way of doing peace work in the Irish situation. Unfortunately, the Glencree Centre had closed down in 1988 and we were busy in getting renewed funding to open it. The final piece of the process jigsaw came together when I was introduced to Professor Herb Kelman, who held the chair of the Middle East Seminar at the Harvard Centre for International Affairs. He had spent twenty years perfecting the problem solving workshop. Every few months he brought together about ten Palestinians and ten Israelis together in a behind-the-scenes unofficial second track process. In the post Six-Day War situation, the workshops helped create the psychological prerequisites for mutual acceptance and the conditions for meaningful negotiations. Kelman believes that "psychological barriers" constitute seventy percent of the problem in resolving identity conflicts. As long as these barriers exist, the parties are locked into rigid assumptions and postures rooted in past history. Kelman warns that overcoming these psychological barriers does not of itself resolve the conflict because that only comes through political negotiation and change.

Political Dialogue Workshops

With my groundwork done and the re-opening of the Glencree Centre in 1994, we could not have timed it better. At the end of August, the IRA announced their cease-fire which was followed quickly in October 1994 by the combined loyalist cease-fire. We held our first political dialogue weekend workshop in October for southern parties. It was a unique occasion for the mainstream political parties to sit in the same room with Sinn Fein in an atmosphere of hope for the future. Since then we have held over 40 workshops and other events at Glencree using the dialogue process model. Over time participants have come from all the political parties in all five parts of Britain and Ireland and benefitted from the opportunity to examine and think with each other on the difficult issues that have acted as roadblocks in the peace process. They have built personal relationships across the parties, created new understandings of each other's political positions and forged networking opportunities that connect people at times of crisis and at different stages of the peace process.

There have been local councillors, policy advisers, party executive members, officers of youth/women's sections and occasionally some parliamentarians. Each workshop has about fourteen to twenty participants, occasionally going up to twenty-eight when all three strands are present (Britain, Northern Ireland and the Republic).

The ultimate test is whether double loop dialogue can help to transform the conflictual relationship between parties. We may never know. The workshops have demonstrated that it is possible to talk with people from the other side without sacrificing their political integrity or it being seen as treacherous. The engagement process also helps party activists to give leadership in developing new thinking within their own party to address the conflict.

I take it that what all men are really after is some form of, perhaps only some formula of, peace.

Joseph Conrad

Everyone wants Peace
Peadar Cremin

Peader Cremin, Ph.D., is the President of Mary Immaculate College of Education in Limerick and a member of the Board of the Irish Peace Institute.

E veryone wants peace. There is a risk that when a cliché, such as this, is repeated often enough, people come to believe that the mantra must be true. But is it? Do most of us really want peace? Or do we just mean that we want some peace or that we want some conditional type of peace? Few in our society bring a pacific viewpoint into the manner in which we care for ourselves, for others, for the animal world or for our environment. Friends and relations may offer a practice ground for peaceful coexistence, but what of relationships with those whom we dislike or fear or do not know and understand? What of the relationships that cross religious, racial and cultural divides? Certain groups may advocate peace and care in aspects of these relationships and thereby win our admiration for their passion and commitment. But violence, terrorism and war all have a place in the societies we have constructed, and from an early age, whether consciously or not, our young are inducted into a violent world. The fact that the world we have constructed is less than a perfect place (and that many of us have, at one point or another, played our part in keeping it that way) should not excuse us from promoting the vision and seeking to construct a more pacific world for all.

As an educationalist, I am interested in how a more peace loving society can be constructed in our schools. Developing an awareness of violence and conflict, promoting the skills of mediation and conflict resolution in these and other settings may seem a long way from the theoretical notion of perfect peace, but even imperfect peace will elude us if the awareness and the skills mentioned remain undeveloped. Educators (including parents and teachers) have constant opportunities to promote awareness and skills in peaceful living in the home, in the school and elsewhere. This does not mean that our children will grow up in totally peaceful settings. There is a risk that you, the reader, may conjure up the product of such an education as some weak and timid but peace loving 'namby pamby'. Our young people cannot be totally shielded from conflict and/or violence (nor would it be necessarily good if they were). In the context of secure, supportive relationships, they need to develop skills in addressing and overcoming the challenges of conflict and of violence. As such, they will grow to adulthood capable of identifying and coping with these forces by addressing them head-on. The experience of doing so will assist them in meeting the challenges of living in a more pacific way in modern society. Studying and practising skills of conflict resolution, conflict management and the art of mediation in the home, in the playground and in the classroom can provide essential experiences in learning to live in better relationships with others. In this way, the individual efforts of parents and teachers can make a contribution to building a more peaceful society, locally as well as globally. The change, which can be wrought by the joint efforts of a great many like-minded people, is inestimable.

When Reason Sleeps
Nora Crowley

Nora Crowley is a Commerce graduate and part-time teacher. She also has a business career and a life long involvement in community work.

S ocieties which are united in a push to achieve prosperity have a dynamism which effectively responds to change, such societies are wary of state intrusion in economic matters as it is suspected that agents of the state are technically conservative and by their training unused to flexible responses to changing market conditions. What is preferred is the U. S. model where the government acts as referee rather than player in economic matters and gives space to the people able to succeed, while providing a safety net through taxation and welfare policies for those who cannot.

For what is freedom without this sense of space? And yet freedom is threatened if within a society there exists an alienated underclass. Brian Barry argues in his powerful book *'Culture and Equality'* that a fair society cannot be sustained over time without a common civic culture committed to some notion of liberal egalitarianism. If a society is divided by conflict, then the whole value system of that culture must be seriously examined if behaviours are to change in an organic and enduring way. And crucial to this examination is a recognition of the fears which divide and cripple. Being in contact with reality is a measure of good health in a society as well as in an individual and where these fears are based on lazy stereotypes, then the old myths must be challenged. However, many of the fears are all too real and it is vital to the interests of any divided community that strong efforts be made to create an infrastructure of justice and an investment in the educational, political and social structures that give every member of society an equal chance to participate.

Basic to any involvement of the whole society is a good educational system. This permits the members to get maximum mileage out of natural ability and enriches all sectors by allowing them to draw on the intelligence of the whole society. A sound education addresses the whole person, body, mind and spirit. It is through the spirit that we develop a sense of connectedness with our environment and with our fellows. Many of the world religions aim at achieving a greater understanding, in the sense of seeing yourself as part of something much bigger, more worthy of respect than you could ever be. Also they challenge egocentricity, the need to dominate others and encourage us to give validity to other people's needs. But not only are we enjoined to love others, we are told to love and respect what we ourselves have to offer, to perfect our talents, to be of maximum benefit to the community in which we work and live.

Democracy insists that power comes from the people. But if this is not just a slogan but a principle to which the political parties give allegiance, then the people must be informed and educated to be intellectually curious. Paine said *"every generation must be free to act for itself as they react to changing circumstances"*. However, such freedom is limited if the whole range of choices are not known, and there is a rigid refusal to accept that circumstances have changed. What is most crippling to a community is an obstinate refusal to change, to look at reality. People cling to old mental maps while what is needed is constant redrafting as they check and recheck the facts against current thinking. 'Get real, man!' is an exhortation of every fresh generation to the one which preceded it. So it can be a genuine disappointment when young people, ignoring their own advice, resort to old arguments and scratch at old sores.

The classic philosophers believed the thing to fear most is the absence of reason. When reason sleeps, the monsters breed and certainly from the Celtic mist have emerged quite a few to disfigure and distort normal civic relations. The best advice for a culture which is divided by conflicting views is to stop hating and to start thinking, to allow people to live with the minimum of confusion and anxiety. In the book *Life, and How to Survive It* Robin Skynner and John Cleese identify a characteristic common to all fundamentalists - they make themselves feel better by attributing all negative and destructive emotions to people of different beliefs, so enjoying the comforting glow of self-justification that results. And yet within their own community people with such strong beliefs can be all that good neighbours should be, friendly, warm, loyal and straight. Regretfully, to those outside the fold, only scornful suspicion is shown. Cleese quotes the simile *"As rare as a Fundamentalist who loves his enemy"*.

A healthy society is an inclusive one. The world and its resources are no longer seen in a feudal way, with rights to ownership being apportioned between loyal subjects to the leader. Economic inclusion ensures that individuals will work for peace. Those who have much to lose are motivated to act responsibly. He who rows the boat or owns the cargo is not likely to scuttle it. Profit as a reward for success in competitive ventures puts control in the hands of those with a proven track record and is a version of natural selection in operation. A man and woman who conform to the Greek ideal of self fulfilment by creating a child, building a house, and planting a tree will see their lives' work continue into the future and will do all in their power to protect it.

In a peaceful society each member submits to the democratically expressed will of the majority. However, it remains the function of government to ensure that minority rights are not infringed and the burden placed on each citizen is reasonable. Basically, it is up to the government to create opportunities and, with a bit of fine-tuning, to allow the people to provide for themselves.

An effective leader is likely to be forward thinking and challenges those who are stuck in old grooves. Essentially he or she must be gifted with powers of communication to be able to sell this expansive vision and to draw on the creativity and problem solving capacity of the majority. Changes can be painful and to compensate for the effort of acquiring new skills the rewards should be proportionate. As technologies become more sophisticated there exists a gap between current practice and what is innovative and it is in the changeover that good management strategies are needed.

There are many levels of influence within any country. A changing culture and value system sees power move between various groupings, capitalists, trade unionists, church authorities, the judiciary, agents of the state, the media. It is in everyone's interest that those controlling important aspects of our lives should be answerable for their actions. It may not always be true that power corrupts, but it certainly brings arrogance and a self-distancing from reality. In a good democratic system, a regular system of elections ensures that the politicians, at least, are answerable for the implementation of their policies and are subjected to a reality check.

There is a need too for other important groupings to be closely monitored and whatever power is vested in them should be used responsibly for the greater good. An open, fair society provides an excellent climate for investment. It welcomes also the countless feiseanna and fairs, sporting occasions, summer schools, marches and parades which follow closely, one succeeding the other all through the summer months. Such life enhancing occasions should create a sense of connection and it is regrettable when they create tensions and are perceived as non-inclusive. The resourceful people who organise these events have already risen to the challenge of de-politicising them but much remains to be done until it is realised that there is much to be gained by an attitude of give and take, of mutual co-operation in community celebration.

To finish with a fable, a good and holy man wished for peace for himself and his community. In the night he had a dream. He was in a place of light surrounded by objects of beauty. He was given to understand that the Creator of All wished him to choose from his abundance. He expressed his desire for peace. It was not to be given directly. Rather he was given a book '*Wisdom*'. His was the task to read it, to internalise it, and then to communicate it to his people. Having received the book he found this message inscribed:

Peaceful are the people who follow
King Solomon's Plan,
And transform with divine wisdom
The mind of every man.

As wisdom guides the enquiring mind
So the blessings increase,
The lands are lands of fruitfulness
And all the place is peace.

Witness to Conflict

John Cushnahan

John Cushnahan has served on the North Belfast City Council, as the Unionist representative in the Northern Ireland Assembly and as the Fine Gael representative for Munster in the European Parliament. His career has spanned across both sides of the border.

B y 2004, my political career will have spanned three decades - half of which will have been spent in the political cauldron of Northern Ireland, the remainder in the Republic of Ireland.   I consider myself fortunate to have enjoyed such a varied and challenging political life, which during its various stages has involved representing the predominantly nationalist North Belfast on Belfast City Council, the unionist constituency of North Down in the Northern Ireland Assembly (Stormont), and since 1989 the traditionally republican and rural province of Munster in the European Parliament.   These experiences have enabled me to gain a valuable insight into the problems of Northern Ireland, distilled from representing both sides of a divided community in Northern Ireland and subsequently becoming involved in political life in the Republic of Ireland. With the benefit of this background, I would like to present my own interpretation of Northern Ireland's recent history leading up to the establishment of the current peace process and its future prospects.

The seeds of conflict in Northern Ireland were sown in the Anglo-Irish Treaty of 1921, which ended hostilities and secured '*de facto*' independence for twenty-six of Ireland's thirty two counties, creating the political entity called Northern Ireland.   This entity contained an in-built Protestant unionist majority but also a substantial minority of Catholics. Over the next forty years the unionist majority entrenched its political position, exclusively retaining all political power and discriminating against the catholic minority. The consistent failure of unionists to treat the catholic minority as fellow citizens on an equal basis resulted in the 'greening' of Northern Ireland's Catholics, driving them to believe the only just settlement they could obtain would be in an 'all-Ireland' arrangement.

The unionist response to the reasonable demands of the Northern Ireland Civil Rights movement in the late 1960s illustrates this point. The birth of the movement was the direct consequence of new educational proposals, based on the Butler Education Act, guaranteeing free access to education, both secondary and third level. Availing of these new opportunities young Catholics were to achieve major academic successes, which had previously been denied them due to economic constraints. This new generation, strengthened by its newly acquired skills and knowledge, was not prepared to accept second class citizenship and, joined by liberal Protestants, they took to the streets to march for basic civil rights. Regrettably, the response of the Unionist government was hostile and the heavy handed partisan policing of the demonstrations took place in the full gaze of the international media. Northern Ireland was no longer a hidden backwater, it was now an international problem.

Encouraged by the hostile approach of officialdom amid rising tensions and escalating fears, street violence emerged in the form of attacks on Catholic areas by extremist loyalist mobs. At the request of leaders in the Catholic community, the British army was sent in to protect Catholic areas. Ironically, within a short period of time the British army were perceived as 'oppressors' by the very people they were sent to protect, an image promoted by the Provisional IRA, who were engaged in nakedly sectarian acts against Northern Ireland Protestants and were responsible for the murder of more Catholics than any other party to the conflict. IRA violence in turn strengthened the loyalist paramilitary organisations such as the Ulster Defence Association (UDA) and the Ulster Volunteer Force (UVF), who were to carry out the worst of the provinces sectarian atrocities.

The introduction of internment without trial in August 1971 plunged Northern Ireland into new depths of despair. Under pressure from the Stormont government, the UK government introduced internment to tackle the escalating violence. This security measure was badly conceived, based upon poor intelligence and despite the two-sided nature of the violence, was exclusively directed against minority areas. Internment and the killing of thirteen innocent civil rights marchers by the British Parachute Regiment on January 30th 1972 (Bloody Sunday) alienated the entire Catholic community overnight, providing a fertile breeding ground for new IRA recruits. Internment was but one in a series of ill fated strategies on the part of successive British administrations. The problem of Northern Ireland was essentially political which required a political response. Unfortunately, the British tendency was to see it as a security problem which tended to exacerbate rather than resolve the problem.

Over the next two decades a number of political initiatives were launched, the most imaginative of these was the Sunningdale Agreement part of which led to a Power Sharing Executive in 1974. The Power Sharing Executive formed the basis of Northern Ireland's first cross-community devolved government. The parallel proposal to set up a Council of Ireland (with limited powers) was used by unionist opponents to undermine the position of the Unionist leader of the Executive, Mr Brian Faulkner. The Executive fell, but the essence of this political experiment was to be resurrected again in the Good Friday Agreement. So striking are the similarities between the two that one leading nationalist politician perceptively described the Good Friday Agreement as "Sunningdale for slow learners". The tragedy was that thousands more of Northern Ireland's citizens were either to die or be maimed during this learning curve for those who in 1974 showed a lamentable lack of political vision.

Following the collapse of the Sunningdale Agreement two further attempts, such as the 1975 Constitutional Convention and the 1980 Atkins Conference, were made by the British Government to fill the political vacuum, however both failed. Throughout this period one felt that the UK government had no clear strategy for the province, so when any initiative ran into problems they abandoned it and fell back upon their policy of containing the situation to an acceptable level of violence.

The 1981 Republican Hunger Strike, in which ten republican prisoners fasted to death, acted as a catalyst, obliging both the British and Irish Governments to work closer together. The intense emotions aroused polarised Northern Ireland politics like nothing before it, or ever since. In its wake Sinn Féin emerged as a major political force, starting with the election of one of the hunger strikers, Bobby Sands, as a Westminster MP. Other hunger strikers were to be successful in a subsequent general election in the Republic of Ireland. Conscious of this electoral threat, the SDLP unfortunately responded to it by resorting to the sterile politics of abstentionism. Like Sinn Féin, they contested elections to the 1982-1986 Assembly but boycotted its proceedings. Matters were also not helped by the deteriorating personal relationship between the UK Prime Minister Margaret Thatcher and the Irish Taoiseach, Charles Haughey, which reached a very low ebb during the Falklands War.

Anglo-Irish relations improved with the election of a new coalition government in the Republic of Ireland led by Dr. Garret Fitzgerald. Despite Mrs. Thatcher's dismissive reaction to the proposals of the New Ireland Forum Report, civil servants from Britain and Ireland worked assiduously together to conceive the Anglo-Irish Agreement. The Agreement, signed on November 15th 1985, was not intended to provide a solution but rather to create a framework within which agreement would be achieved. Under its terms the Irish Government were to be given a say in the internal affairs of Northern Ireland and this precipitated Unionist anger. Unlike previous initiatives, it could not be brought down by Unionists and this was one of its major strengths. On the debit side, its inherent weakness was that on many occasions the two governments, instead of working together would act as surrogates - the Irish Government representing northern nationalists and the British Government representing the unionists. Instead of Anglo Irish Ministerial meetings being intergovernmental in nature and above Northern Ireland's internal problems on many occasions it became an extension of them.

Over time the emergence of new personalities were to constitute individual but essential parts of a complex political jigsaw. In the absence of any single piece, the jigsaw would never have been completed and possibly agreement would have been further away than ever.

John Major was a more conciliatory individual than his predecessor and co-operating with his Irish counterpart, Albert Reynolds, provided a launching pad for the peace process, signing the Downing Street Declaration on December 15th 1993. This had been preceded by a series of complex negotiations among the Northern Ireland parties. Reynolds was to be a key figure. Major trusted him and the relationship was central to delivering an agreement. The Major-Reynolds efforts were to be rewarded by Republican and Loyalist cease-fires within the next twelve months.

Fine Gael leader John Bruton succeeded Albert Reynolds at the head of a three party coalition government. Deputy Prime Minister and Minister for Foreign Affairs Dick Spring ensured continuity having held the same position under Reynolds. However John Bruton's courageous inclusive approach was to provide a new essential ingredient in the process. Unlike previous Irish Premiers, he believed that the role of the Irish Government should not simply be to represent northern nationalists, but that it also had an equal responsibility to northern unionists. This marked a new and welcome departure for which he was unfairly criticised by narrow minded nationalist politicians, earning him the insulting title of 'John Unionist'. I firmly believe that his approach was critical in changing the attitudes of Northern Ireland's Unionists. Without this happening, it is debatable whether or not they would have embarked upon the path which eventually led to the Good Friday Agreement.

The replacement of John Major and John Bruton by Tony Blair and Bertie Ahern respectively also brought new advantages and consolidated the efforts of the players that preceded them. The new British premier made Northern Ireland a priority and enjoyed an excellent working relationship with the Irish Taoiseach, whose skills as a conciliator were instrumental in persuading the unionists and Sinn Fein to move towards an agreement. In tandem with these Anglo-Irish developments, the role of US President Bill Clinton cannot be overestimated. Despite the popular perception in Ireland, the Irish issue was of little importance on the US political agenda. To become involved carried more negatives than positives. Thankfully this did not deter Bill Clinton. Not only did he personally immerse himself in the affairs of Northern Ireland, he committed senior members of his Administration in the search for a permanent peace, particularly Senator George Mitchell. The appointment of the latter was a stroke of genius as his involvement was to prove pivotal.

Alongside the many positive inputs from London, Dublin and Washington, the efforts of the north's politicians were the most important. The commitment and tenacity of John Hume, especially his decision to enter dialogue with Sinn Fein/IRA in the face of strident and unjustified personal criticism; the political courage of David Trimble; the willingness of Gerry Adams and loyalist paramilitary leaders to choose political dialogue instead of violence coupled with efforts of those who toiled for reconciliation combined together to deliver the Good Friday Agreement on that historic day of April 10th 1998. The award of the Nobel Peace Prize to John Hume and David Trimble was well deserved. Senator George Mitchell encapsulated their joint achievement accurately and succinctly when he said *"Without John Hume, there would not have been a peace process, without David Trimble, there would not have been an agreement".*

Three years on the Good Friday Agreement remains in place. Although it has been put under considerable strain because of a number of crises, it has managed to overcome them so far. However, the biggest single threat to its continued survival comes from David Trimble's own party. If the anti-agreement faction inside the Ulster Unionist Party were to succeed in overthrowing his leadership, the current phase in the peace process would be brought to a speedy end. If he is to survive it is essential that the paramilitary organisations, especially the Provisional IRA, deliver something of substance with regard to the decommissioning of paramilitary weapons. A failure to do so will result in David Trimble becoming the Brian Faulkner of 2001.

While there are many problems that still need to be overcome before we can be totally confident that we are moving towards permanent peace in Ireland, I remain hopeful about the future. Whatever current ones exist and whatever unforeseen ones may appear in the future, they will only temporarily halt the process. They will not prove fatal.

There has already been too much pain, too much suffering, too much unnecessary death and destruction. As so much has already been invested to prevent this ever reoccurring, I have every confidence that the ordinary people of Ireland, North and South, will maintain pressure on their political representatives, either in or out of governments, to ensure that the peace process does not unravel.

There is one thing stronger than all the armies in the world, and
that is an idea whose time has come.

Victor Hugo

Soldiering for Peace
Colm Doyle

Colonel Colm Doyle is the School Commandant of the Irish Defence Forces United Nations Training School, which is part of the Military College at the Curragh. He was commissioned an infantry officer in 1966 and has served in a wide variety of command and staff appointments throughout his career. His military service abroad includes tours of duty with the United Nations in Cyprus, the Middle East and the Lebanon where he commanded the 82nd Irish Battalion in 1997/98. He served with the OSCE as head of the European Community Monitor Mission (ECMM) in Bosnia in 1991 and returned there as Lord Peter Carrington's Personal Representative in 1992. He is a former commander of the 12th Infantry Battalion in Limerick and Director of Public Relations for the Defence Forces. Colonel Doyle holds a Masters Degree in International Studies from the University of Limerick.

In February 1999 I was invited to deliver a lecture in Geneva to a gathering of international non-governmental organisations (NGO's) undertaking a diploma course in Humanitarian Assistance. During the course of my delivery I mentioned that all my overseas experience in the 35 years of military service with the Irish Defence Forces was solely on peace operations as a peacekeeper. I was approached at the end of my lecture by an elderly German who expressed astonishment that as a professional soldier I had never engaged in direct combat. As he himself put it "I never realised there was another way".

The Irish Defence Forces have been practising "the other way" for more than forty three years. From the deployment of fifty military officers to the United Nations Observer Group in Lebanon in 1958 our involvement in peacekeeping has been continuous. In those forty three years since then Irish soldiers have completed over 50,000 tours of duty, mostly of six months duration in over 37 United Nations operations spread across forty countries world-wide. The Congo, Sinai, Cyprus, Cambodia, Kuwait, Angola, Namibia, Yugoslavia, Kosovo and East Timor are just some of the many places that have become familiar to Irish peacekeepers. Mediation, negotiation and gentle persuasion have become the weapons of the peacekeeper and in truth the Irish soldier has become as good as any and better than many at their use. Over twenty of the United Nations operations undertaken by Irish personnel have been unarmed missions where the emphasis has been on observation and reporting, liaison, use of good offices and facilitating discussion rather than on confrontation. The bedrock of these operations are based on consent, non-use of force (except in self-defence) and impartiality.

Many UN missions have occurred since 1988 when there was an explosion in the demand for peacekeeping operations brought about by the end of the cold war and the demise of Communism. In addition to serving with the many missions of the United Nations, the Defence Forces have had overseas commitment to peace missions conducted by the European Union and the Organisation for Security and Co-operation in Europe (OSCE). The futility of war has been evidenced by our troops who have been committed to humanitarian work in relief of some of the appalling suffering endured by the people of Somalia and Rwanda.

An observation from the above statistics is that Ireland has given generously to international peacekeeping missions over a long period of time and for which there has been a cost. A total of 82 soldiers have lost their lives while on duty abroad in the service of peace. For this service the Defence Forces have acquired a wide range of experience in peace operations which have been established to increase security or to relieve the acute human suffering which is an inevitable by-product of armed conflict.

In the context of the UN Charter, peacekeeping is paradoxical, as the word 'peacekeeping' does not appear anywhere in the text. Indeed it was probably an unknown concept when the founding fathers drafted their plans for new collective security in the immediate aftermath of World War Two. Peacekeeping would seem to be a contradiction in terms for a soldier who, after all, is primarily trained in the art of war. Yet, it was the former UN Secretary General Hammarskjold who said that "peacekeeping is not a suitable job for soldiers, yet they are the only ones who can do it". In terms of definition, peacekeeping is a deployment of a peace operation in the field, hitherto with the consent of the parties concerned, normally involving military and/or police personnel and frequently civilians as well. Peacekeeping is a technique that expands the possibility for both the prevention of conflict and the making of peace.

The Defence Forces have amassed a wide range of skills and experience in peacekeeping since 1958 and are keen to remain abreast of developments. To this end a special military school was established in 1993 named the United Nations Training School, Ireland (UNTSI). It is a constituent school of the Military College with the principal aim of ensuring that the Defence Forces training for peacekeeping would be of the highest standards in all aspects of today's complex peace support operations. The mission of the school therefore is to study developments in peacekeeping in all its forms: to develop peacekeeping doctrine and to conduct training courses and seminars on peacekeeping in order to ensure high standards of performance by Defence Forces personnel on peacekeeping missions. The school also offers training courses in peace operations to foreign military students. For example, in June of this year it conducted a United Nations Military Observer and Staff Officer Course (UNMOSOC) for military officers from 21 countries throughout the five continents. This is the seventh such course conducted by the school.

Soldiers are trained in the profession of arms and the theory of war. Yet for the Irish soldier the only real application of his profession abroad over many decades has been the application of peace. It is a reputation that has brought much credit to the Defence Forces and one for which I believe they should be justifiably proud.

Peace at any Price
Ruth Dudley Edwards

> *Sometime academic, teacher, marketing executive and civil servant, Ruth Dudley Edwards has been a freelance writer since 1979. Ruth was born and brought up in Dublin, was a student at University College Dublin, a post-graduate at Cambridge University and now lives in London. She is an historian and prize-winning biographer (the James Tait Black Memorial Prize for Victor Gollancz: a biography). Since 1993, Ruth has written seriously and/or frivolously for almost every national newspaper in the Republic of Ireland and the United Kingdom and appears frequently on radio and television in Ireland, the UK and on the BBC World Service. Ruth feels both Irish and English and greatly enjoys being part of both cultures.*

"*We love peace, as we abhor pusillanimity*" wrote the nineteenth-century writer Douglas Jerrold, "*but not peace at any price. There is a peace more destructive of the manhood of living man than war is destructive of his material body. Chains are worse than bayonets*".

Most of us believe that in theory, yet our abhorrence of violence and war so often causes us to forget that what is important is to decide on what price as a society we can afford to pay and not be bounced into increasing it. There is not a patriotic, constitutional politician in Ireland who in the early, or even the mid, 1990s would have contemplated paying the price to Sinn Fein/IRA that has been paid by two frightened liberal governments on behalf of the unfortunate peoples they represent. They have appeased, appeased and appeased in the name of peace, by recklessly upping the price.

Appeasement of the warmonger has never worked in human history - not in personal relationships and not in inter-tribal or international relationships: give the monster a cookie, and he asks for a glass of milk. We know that in theory, yet though in Ireland there were just a few hundred warmongers, our governments caved in every time they threatened. The result has been to strengthen terrorism, increase sectarianism and corrupt two democracies.

Why did a small group of terrorists who were weak militarily, electorally and financially succeed in making fools of two sovereign governments? Well, *inter alia*, because the terrorists were absolutely clear about what they wanted, while the governments just wanted the violence to stop and - through ignorance and naivete - had no idea whom they were dealing with and what they were doing. Both too had swallowed John Hume's disastrous dictum that peace should be made from the extremes in rather than from the centre out - as happened in South Africa.

Because Britain owned Northern Ireland and the Republic claimed it did, neither had treated the province like a foreign country. So over the decades they had sent no diplomats to discover what the natives were like, to immerse themselves in the various cultures and send back to London or Dublin sensitive, informed and realistic reports. And since the voters of Northern Ireland could not elect either British or Irish governments, politicians had no incentive to get to know the people, so neither British nor Irish politicians had the remotest clue about the cast of mind of a Shankill Road window-cleaner, a Falls Road barman, a County Tyrone Orange shopkeeper, a republican assassin from Crossmaglen, a Catholic member of the RUC or a Taig-hating Portadown loyalist. Nor did the

Dublin and Whitehall officials who formulated the policies and drafted the documents, determined that some settlement be reached, however flawed and however expensive.

With the honourable exception of John Bruton, who believed that the duty of the government of the Irish Republic was to serve the interests of all the people of Northern Ireland, Dublin governments meekly followed instructions, first from John Hume, and then, as the republican star rose, Gerry Adams. Betraying our nationalist characteristic of wishful thinking, they believed passionately that if you believed in peace enough, it would happen. Obediently, they accepted the view that unionists were a problem for the British and could thus be ignored, though they demanded too that Britain be as neutral as Ireland was partisan. The British, for the most part, accepted the principle of neutrality and operated on the presumption that if you are nice to terrorists, they will be nice to you. That unfortunate misconception was embodied in the approach of Mo Mowlam and was what led to the release of the terrorist prisoners without as much as a pike being given up in return.

With media collusion, peace became the mantra that made it an actual virtue to allow the wool to be pulled over your eyes. To suggest that the leaders of Sinn Fein/IRA were cynical, brutal opportunists was to be anti-peace. To criticise the peace process was to be anti-peace. Soon, to draw attention to mutilation, graft, electoral fraud, intimidation, racketeering and even murder was to be anti-peace. And since the violent set the agenda, in every crisis paramilitaries were paid off again rather than faced down. And with every payment, they grew stronger.

The fundamental problem in the island of Ireland is tribal, and tribalism thrives on ignorance. Whether you want a peaceful Northern Ireland within the United Kingdom or as part of a United Ireland, this is obtainable only if the ordinary people can get on together. I have the greatest respect for the peace groups who have made the effort – with little, if no, support from their own tribes – to reach out to people of different traditions and painstakingly try to learn about them. Had the two governments done likewise, while taking a principled line with paramilitaries, we might now have the beginnings of a proper peace. As it is, appeasement has left us with triumphalist republicanism, nihilistic loyalism, sullen unionism and nervous nationalism.

Peace is a Process - Not an Event

Robin Eames

The Most Reverend Robert Henry Alexander Eames is the Archbishop of Armagh, Primate of all Ireland and Metropolitan. Educated at Methodist College, Belfast; Belfast Royal Academy; and the Queen's University of Belfast. In 1960, he graduated with an LLB (Hons) and received his Ph.D. in 1963. He holds Honorary Doctorates in Law and Divinity from QUB, Trinity College Dublin, Cambridge, Lancaster and Aberdeen Universities. Ordained in St. Clement's Belfast in 1963, he was made a Bishop in 1975. Elected Bishop of Derry and Raphoe on 9 May 1975, he was subsequently elected Bishop of Down and Dromore five years later in April 1980. On 7 February 1986, the House of Bishops elected him Archbishop of Armagh, Primate of All Ireland and Metropolitan. He became a life peer in 1995.

I have often reflected on the ways our contemporary society uses language. In my own experience there are several words which have become overworked, and at times undervalued, simply because their use has represented convenient cover for inadequate thinking or shallow reasoning. Two in particular spring to mind: reconciliation and peace. In the last decade those words have become the most frequently used in Northern Ireland - and on many occasions appear to have lost their real impact because of their familiarity.

What do we mean by reconciliation and what do we mean by peace? Is reconciliation a fact which we will recognise when it arrives in this society and will it be denoted by evidence which is emphatic and non-debatable? Is peace likewise a situation which will suddenly break out as an absence of conflict? What is the real difference between a journey towards reconciliation and peace and a moment in time when everyone will have been reconciled and everyone will be at total peace with each other? Wherein lies the positive - wherein lies the negative?

Surely the truth is that reconciliation and peace represent a process and both are in fact relative terms?

I recall a visit to a school when a sixth former asked me: *"How will I recognise the day I wake up and reconciliation will have happened?"* There is no easy answer, is there?

I read human history as a series of co-related processes in which human-kind has moved in several directions, influenced by varying pressures both positive and negative, until either the world has found a better alternative and changed direction or has become satisfied with the results of its endeavours until a further challenge has been presented. European history in particular has surely borne testimony to these developments.

In pluralist Ireland we are on a journey. For behind us are the idyllic days of saints and scholars. Out of division, hatred, suspicion and inter-community strife we are living through days when a new set of values is being worked out. Those values are to do with basic understanding of difference, basic questions of community identity and searching issues of coming to terms with differing political, religious, cultural and economic aspirations. Violence, so near the surface of Irish history, has failed. Political dialogue remains a tender plant. Religion has been compelled to take stock of its position and ask to what degree it has contributed to division. The Churches have had to recognise their role in the problem while not yet fully understanding their role in finding long-term solutions. In each instance the real lesson for those who participate is to recognise that this is now a pluralist Ireland and that Ireland, like them, is engaged on a journey of process.

The real question then remains - what is the destination of that journey?

I am convinced that the real completion of this process will be an Ireland at peace with itself - not because there is an absence of tension, for tension itself can be positive but at peace with difference through equality, respect, tolerance and dignity. I see the first tentative signs of this emerging in these days. I pray that this generation, perhaps the first to recognise what the real questions are, will also be the first to benefit from the genuine accommodation of difference.

For a Christian so much of this is bound up in the Gospel imperative. In the pluralism of modern Ireland the Church may have to work out a new dynamic if it is to be truly relevant to the needs and desires of this island. Until then surely the most relevant and eternal comment must be *'Father forgive....'*.

He drew a circle that shut me out,
Heretic, rebel, a thing to flout.
But love and I had the wit to win:
We drew a circle that took him in!

Edwin Markham

Towards a Better Understanding
Denis Faul

Denis Faul, born in County Louth, is a leading campaigner against alleged ill-treatment of people detained by the security forces in Northern Ireland. Father Faul spent 40 years at St Patrick's Academy, Dungannon, the last fifteen of them as Principal, before moving to Carrickmore, County Tyrone as Parish Priest in 1998. He first attracted public attention in 1969 when he criticised the Northern Ireland judicial system and the actions of the police and army. He was chaplain to the Maze Prison during the H-block hunger strikes, which he strongly opposed, nevertheless urging the government to make concessions to prisoners. Although an outspoken critic of IRA violence, he called for the early release of young and long-term prisoners as a means of diffusing tension in Northern Ireland.

John F. Kennedy said that in all the countries of the world, 30% of the people declare themselves against everything! Perhaps in Ireland we could register 50%!

An Irishman was ship wrecked in the Pacific Ocean. He swam for 50 miles to a deserted island. As he hauled himself up on the shore, he said *"If there is a government here I'm again' it !"*.

The enemy of better understanding is the *Tongue*. The solution is: let the politician, the clergy, the media, the organisation put their carping tongues completely and verifiably beyond use! Gearr do Theanga nó gearfaidh sé do scornach ! - Actions speak louder than words.

Not to reply to the bigoted remark, the sectarian jibe, to the offensive slogans, the party tribal tunes, are actions which lead to peace and better understanding. It takes two to make a fight and if one party refuses to join in the hostilities, the other party is left with his aggressive mouth open.

Win an argument and lose a friend, even a wife !

Remember that reality is not 'them and us', only *us* - it is a we - we are the solution.

I remember in 1972, I was in Washington for hearings concerning the Northern Ireland troubles. Later in New York, we had an interview with two men from the New York Times, both Jews, although one was called Mooney! We ranted on about the Catholic community and the Protestant community. Finally, they interrupted, *"There is only one community in Northern Ireland - the people who live there, learn to live together".* I was so taken aback that I forgot to say, *"What about the Jews and Arabs in Israel?"*

Bring Clinton, Bush, Blair, Bertie, Mitchell. O.K., O. K., good PR surface stuff, but unless the people who live here look at each other, love each other, help each other with charity and concern, say *little,* do a *lot* for each other. We have failed to understand the sense of loss, of victim-hood, of the other half of the community. Even after seven years of partial cease-fire, three years of the Agreement, we are unable to stand in the other person's shoes, or look through his spectacles, to sympathise, to suffer with 'sun-pathein'.

We have not the *moral courage* to step out of our tribe, to go to the other side, to see suffering humans there and to help them, however we have plenty of physical courage to kill, wound and maim persons and drive them from their homes. I recall a hateful expression I was ashamed to hear from my fellow Catholics, *"I shot the uniform, not the man!"* But there was a man or a woman inside the uniform with a father, mother, maybe a spouse and young children. No sympathy, no empathy, no love?

Courtesy, generosity, co-operation, give and take, these are the essential qualities of a fruitful dialogue.

Take the manager of a large business, or take the headmaster of a large school with a staff of fifty or more. How to manage without conflict? Remember **"Harmony** *is more important than efficiency, because* **harmony** *promotes* **efficiency.** *"*

A headmaster, a director has to listen to a lot of criticism, sometimes useful, often ill-natured and malicious. He is well paid to listen to attacks, to smile and to keep his temper, remembering that he is paid more than his critics because he has to listen to them!

So it is also in the political world. We have to listen to hurtful and wounding talk, but we must not reply in kind. I remember hearing what Mick O'Dwyer said of his management of the many champion Kerry teams, *"I cannot afford to fall out with Bomber Liston or Pat Spillane, because the County Kerry people need them"*.

If I cannot understand my neighbour, I cannot understand myself. If I fight with my neighbour it is because I dislike myself. I knew a brainy man who could not manage except by fear. People said, *"He must dislike himself intensely"*.

Finally, may I quote the Graffiti star of Belfast, the Pope! He said, *"If you want to reform the world, begin with yourself and your own backyard!"*

I have met many assistants from France, Germany, and Italy helping language students in Northern Ireland. They all say how kind and welcoming the Protestants and the Catholics are, but they find it strange that A loves C and B loves C, but A and B distrust each other! We see the Europeans as gifts, but we see each other as threats, not as gifts. In community building here there are too many *weakest links*.

Milestones and Lessons
Eirwin Harbottle

> *In her time, Eirwen Harbottle has been an actress, puppeteer, flower farmer and radio/TV newscaster - in Cape Town, Cairo, Jerusalem and Nicosia. In her second marriage to Brigadier Michael Harbottle, she assisted him in various activities relating to refugees, UN peacekeeping and disarmament. Together they created the Centre for International Peacebuilding to facilitate initiatives designed to bring together people sharing common interests, especially across the East-West Cold War divide. Now in her widowhood, she continues this work, with particular concern for the involvement of both young and the military in environmental and peacebuilding activities. She is Co-ordinator of the Worldwide Consultative Association of Retired Generals and Admirals.*

S pringing from a life frequently disrupted by conflict:

Cyprus, 1931: Rioters burn down Government House. British soldiers billeted in our downstairs hall, protecting the Bank of which my father is Manager. Perplexity for a fearful 10 year old: why are we so hated? Isn't Cyprus British, alongside all other blobs of red on the world map?

World War 2, 1941: Evacuation from Cyprus, threatened by German occupation following fall of Crete. Leaving home, maybe forever. Just one suitcase - what to pack? Crushing loneliness of Cape Town tea party 'for the evacuees'. Longing to belong engenders a lasting empathy for all refugees.

Jerusalem, 1946: First baby elects to arrive as a gun battle rages outside hospital - Jewish fighters blowing up adjacent central gaol. Chaotic city reduced to standstill. Where's the logic promising the same land to two opposing peoples? Impossible that holy Jerusalem might someday be shared harmoniously by three religions?

Cyprus, 1950's: Violence stalks…Greek Cypriot EOKA campaigners raise perplexities about 'terrorists' or 'freedom fighters'. As a flower farmer, making wreaths for young British soldiers, becomes soul-searing. Why should they die when clearly so soon Cyprus will win independence…?

Cyprus, 1960's: Violence goes intercommunal, uncomfortably subjecting our hilltop flower farm to volleys of bullets and bawled invective from Greeks and Turks occupying surrounding mountain positions. Blessed UN peacekeepers introduce miraculous calm, allowing life to continue relatively normally. Never forget how much I owe the UN! A radio newscaster under former colonial then new republican regimes, wryly I observe that propaganda seems designed to bolster one's own convictions; seldom to examine all aspects of conflict.

Vienna, 1970: Now remarried to a soldier who found a new military purpose in UN service. Taking early retirement, he'd written the first thoughtful book about problems and attitudes in UN peacekeeping (*The Impartial Soldier*, Michael Harbottle, OUP 1970). Now heading peacekeeping team for International Peace Academy's first Vienna seminar, linking disciplines of peacekeeping (military), peacemaking (diplomats), peace theory and peaceful social change in our first experience of holistic thinking. Here are serving generals, diplomats, NGO executives, priests and peaceniks engaged in a ferment of exchanges, often through role play, probing fundamental causes of 'unpeace', whether stemming from economic or wider social injustices. Learn from Johan Galtung the subtle differences between 'manifest', 'structural' and 'cultural' violence.

London, 1970's: My mentor Richard Hauser's maxim blazoned above door of his Centre for Human Rights and Responsibilities: *"Responsibility is the only Socially Maturing Factor"* - Later move next door to help the Kurds where I encounter lethal nature of oil politics. Subsequently help British Council for Aid to Refugees in resettlement of Vietnamese Boat People; sad to encounter many colonialist attitudes...

1980's: Assist Michael in World Disarmament Campaign, preparing for UN 2nd Special Session on Disarmament . (Shamefully ignorant; never knew there was a 1st SSD). Wonderful new friends but find certain unpeace in the peace movement?!

October 1981: persuade reluctant WDC colleagues to sponsor a youth musical demonstrating what the kids think. *("Ridiculous! What do children know about disarmament?" "Much more than you think....!")* Fortuitous cancellation at Albert Hall on last night of Disarmament Week secures our premiere of 'Peace Child'! Watching, Séan McBride says, *"You must take this to the UN!"* What a vision!

1983: Michael and I create the Centre for International Peacebuilding to facilitate/initiate projects designed to further co-operation between people sharing common concerns - especially across East/West divide. Pass on

£1,000 donation received for 'confidence building' to Birmingham University to facilitate visit of child psychologist to Budapest's Peto Institute where Russian psychology achieved remarkable success educating brain damaged children. (This will lead to the creation of the British Institute for Conductive Education with Princess Di as onetime Patron. No better use for £1,000.)

1984: Volunteer to be honorary rapporteur to 'Generals for Peace and Disarmament' - Michael's initiative to create dialogue between retired senior officers from NATO/WTO countries. Over next five years fascinated to watch their developing rapport. All know the folly and waste of war. But no support from western governments.

Gradually realise inadequacy of 'single issue' thinking in grappling with problems of peace-and-conflict. Art classes ram this home: we must draw connecting lines and see angles between them to get the truth onto paper - a compelling discipline which suddenly I realise applies equally to global issues. For example considering refugees, first 'connecting line' surely must be arms trade, directly fostering wars, wholesale displacement of people and widening gap between rich and poor. Am told by Russian teacher that Gorbachev's 'perestroika' means *"clarify what you think: is it relevant to present needs? If not, how must we change our thinking?"* - another important intellectual challenge. Then remember Einstein: *"we cannot solve problems with the thinking which caused them..."*

Peace Child kids understand! They are now rewriting books for UN agencies in global kid-speak.

1997: Suddenly widowed, I resolve to continue Michael's work. Am now Co-ordinator of renamed 'Worldwide Consultative Association of Retired Generals and Admirals' (a UN accredited NGO). www. wcarga.org website carries details of their 'virtual library', uniquely collating material on conflict prevention, plus anecdotal lessons of failures and successes. Must include military - and youth - in peacebuilding.

In a nutshell: seek ways to promote collaboration between often unlikely people. Also remember: water always flows around obstacles barring its way...

Working now to demonstrate integrated nature of global security in which economic, environmental, military/political and psychological/ethical/ spiritual issues must be viewed as inescapably intertwined.

You've got to have something to eat
and a little love in your life before you can hold still
for any damn body's sermon on how to behave.

Billie Holiday

The Uncertain Balance of Present and Future

Agnes Harrington

Agnes Harrington is an academic who has worked in several British universities and published on political and social affairs.

I want to draw attention to configurations of development and communication and to problems of neighbourly coexistence and insecurity in the midst of the unevenly prosperous present and the imponderable uncertainties of the future.

A plate glass world of rich and poor

We dwell in a globalised world, especially in communications, in which the aspirations of nearly all peoples are growing. Yet rich countries with their superb technology are consuming the world's energy and materials at a rapid pace. They can maintain current consumption levels because only a small section of the world is using energy and materials on their scale and at their speed. But in a generation or so great countries like China, India and Brazil, not to mention others, are going to consume many more resources. Yet with present technology, even as it improves, and existing resources it is going to be impossible, whilst safeguarding the planet, to cater for the interests of all those who cherish rising aspirations.

Structural blockages combined with resource competition could quickly lead to strains between regions and between states, damaging communication between groups and breaking down a trust that is crucial to the international system. In consequence, a central challenge for those who control technology is to find out how to increase and to share global resources. For that there is no alternative to carrying out the research that will enable our contemporaries to use existing resources more frugally, to work on value added approaches, and to create new resources in skills, equipment and materials that can be expanded and made available for global use. Coming generations may blame us most of all because we have short changed the investment in research that envisages future shortages. Unfortunately the future has no votes.

The presence of weapons of mass destruction

Competition for scarce resources and poorly controlled technological exploitation can come together in a malign convergence. We live at a time when methods of attack have moved well ahead of conceivable methods of defence. We have in nuclear, chemical and biological weapons - weapons of mass destruction - an inordinate capacity to devastate entire regions and possibly most of the planet. There is no way of avoiding such destruction, or at least partial destruction, unless we can get states to co-operate with one another. For that reason committed opinion formers within the nuclear powers may play a crucial role in bringing dangers sensitively to the attention of their governments. Politicians have to be persuaded that we possess technology that requires patterns of global government and forms of international co-operation that we have up to now not been ready for psychologically or politically. Yet we have had at least one nuclear generation to get ready psychologically; and we have in measure not used it. We can't afford not to move politically very soon. New American defence measures have recently been proposed against 'rogue states'. The real dangers lie however among the newly great military powers - India, Pakistan and China - and siege states such as Israel. Deterrence that was bi-lateral has worked, if precariously, for a time. Deterrence that has become multi-lateral creates a much more dangerous security situation.

Anomalies of history-international relations without safeguards

History has left behind political anomalies of all sorts that have taken on different shapes as modernising technology and the structures of colonial occupations have altered relations between groups. A corrosive problem is that many groups find themselves within the same political structures as groups they do not particularly care for or trust. Among the recalcitrant are Tamils, Kurds, Tibetans, Sahelians, Nigerians and Congolese of all ethnic groups, Hutus and Tutsis; and in a shock to Europeans who a generation ago thought that ethnic problems belonged only to the Third World we have Romanians, Hungarians, Croats and Serbs awkwardly out of place, Russians stranded in Latvia and Estonia as well as many other places on the periphery of the old Tsarist empire, and dissatisfied Albanians, Irish nationalists, Basques and others. We also see problems between states in the wake of colonial carve up and technological change - the Kashmir issue between two nuclear powers is a festering example but others exist; and there are bound to be more in the making, not to mention the existing politics of the Middle East in which Israeli power and insecurity and Arab claims and revanchism blend into a malign mixture. For such reasons we need to work out mediation approaches, secure arms control agreements, and devise methods of raising peace-making and peace-keeping forces. These initiatives have to depend on powerful states with leverage as well as on smaller states of good standing. The UN is currently working on these issues but there is a long way to go. We cannot afford any longer to look upon war as a recurring misfortune but need to see it as a solvable problem.

Endemic poverty

Most people in the world are still desperately poor; and in a see-through world they know they are poor. It is tempting to blame Western countries for sustaining poverty, but it is still the case that much progress and many aspirations have come from contact with the region which initiated technological modernisation. Some twenty years ago in a survey of Nigerian student attitudes I asked if on balance colonisation had been a good or a bad thing. In their answers they split evenly, something that doesn't easily happen mathematically in a survey. In any case what I really want to say here are two things: first, poverty continues in developing countries mostly for reasons internal to them: they are short of skills, and even more so they are short of social attitudes and structures of a kind that developed in the West through a slow and long familiarity with technology. Second, prosperous countries cannot avoid the challenge of world poverty, disease and lack of education, partly for reasons of our common humanity, partly to offset future wars of resources, and partly to increase general prosperity through increased skills and greater purchasing power.

Against a history of colonisation and the contemporary internal problems of development, it is not easy for outsiders to collaborate in development. Yet there is no sensible alternative to working together with poorer countries to enable them to improve internally in political, administrative and economic ways, including safeguarding human rights. The problem is that governments in prosperous countries that are themselves beset by their own short-term problems are little motivated to improve foreign aid because their political audiences are more easily stirred by immediate compassion than by long-term justice; and Western peoples generally remain impervious to future and only dimly visible issues of security.

The presence of poverty within rich states

Within many rich countries there are not just pockets but swathes of poverty: the U.S. and Britain are cases in point where some one-fourth of families with children live below a recognisable poverty level. Such poverty becomes complicated also in some countries in which through migration there is a new ethnic mix; and this mix is aggravated by unemployment and discrimination. If highly developed countries want communities with a sense of common good, they cannot permit situations of poverty and discrimination to endure.

Conclusion

My theme has been an unevenly global world, the dislocations of a powerful and pervasive technology in resource allocation and defence, the awkward proximity of new and old neighbours, and the glimpses of prosperity and poverty through a transmitting and resistant plate glass transparence. My personal belief is that we do not have all the time in the world to deal with these issues. We may suffer great loss in one way or another if we do not - and are not seen to do so - set about them quickly and honestly.

Let them enjoy their sport in the park; but it is only a shadow to that pleasure that I find in Plato. The pleasures of the senses pass quickly; but those of the mind are ever with us.

Lady Jane Grey

Chorus - The Cure at Troy
Seamus Heaney

Educated at St Columb's College, Derry and Queens University Belfast. He held teaching posts in Dublin, then Belfast, and the University of California, Berkeley. He was Professor of Poetry at Oxford from 1989-94 and in 1984 he was named Boylston Professor of Rhetoric at Harvard. He is a recipient of the Nobel Peace Prize for Literature.

Human beings suffer.
They torture one another.
They get hurt and get hard.
No poem or play or song.
Can fully right a wrong.
Inflicted and endured.

History says, Don't hope
On this side of the grave,
But then, once on a lifetime
The longed-for tidal wave
Of justice can rise up
And hope and history rhyme.

So hope for a great sea-change
On the far side of revenge.
Believe that a farther shore
Is reachable from here.
Believe in miracles
And cures and healing wells.

Call miracle self-healing,
The utter self-revealing
Double-take of feeling
If there's fire on the mountain
And lightning and storm
And a god speaks from the sky

That means someone is hearing
The outcry and the birth-cry
Of new life at its term.
It means once in a lifetime
That justice can rise up
And hope and history rhyme.

I Hate Peaceniks

Mark Patrick Hederman

Mark Patrick Hederman is a monk of Glenstal Abbey, Limerick, in Ireland.

My title is from a T-shirt. In the early seventies a friend of mine attended a meeting organised by peace lovers in Trinity College Dublin. They were hoping to end the troubles in the North. They invited representatives of the Northern Unionist viewpoint, Sinn Féin/IRA and other colour parties on the spectrum between bright orange and verd-antique. At one point during the meeting a young bespectacled youth wearing tennis shoes and a long mohair scarf, with a cultivated accent [the youth, that is, not the scarf] was assuring the audience from the podium that he was Irish actually.

"Get off the stage or we'll kneecap you" came the ominous heckle from the pits. He carried on, ignoring the taunts.

They carried on also: *"Get off the stage or we'll kneecap you, and we'll kneecap the mother that bore you!"*

The speaker decided to silence them with pathos.

"Actually, my mother died quite tragically recently, and we have just returned from burying her".

(Pause)

"Well, we'll dig her up out of the grave and we'll kneecap her!"

It is as if the lovers of violence and the promoters of peace were different species. There is a Grand Canyon between the doves and the hawks. There is a body language, an idiom, a vocabulary, a code of conduct, a ceremonial which are antithetical to each other. Vatican II in the Catholic Church with its introduction of 'the kiss of peace' during Mass added fuel to the dual bonfires. Orgies of loveydovery on the sunny side; gutters full of gawk on the shadow side.

It is comparatively easy to build a pagoda of peace for the converted. Everyone wears flowers, sings songs, smiles and links arms as we meet together to confirm each other in the belief that Beatrix Potter rules OK. Beat your swords into ploughshares. Your nuclear warheads into palaces of peace. We attend one another's conferences; march up and down our avenues for peace; recite creeds, publish manifestos, vision statements, five-year plans. It is a diet of do-goodery for the chorus in the chicken coop. While the foxes sharpen warheads and gnash teeth.

Peace is not a theory or manifesto, not a creed or code. It is a deed that is done. While others search for the politician of the century in Ireland, I would prefer to seek out the people on the ground who made things happen. The person who made a dent in the 'peace' scenario over the last half century, to my way of thinking is the 'entrepreneurial peace-maker'.

The 'entrepreneurial peace-maker' quite simply believes in people. She or he will not accept that people are naturally hostile to one another. If they are, it is because someone or something is preventing them from being what they are by nature: folkophiles. People were made to love people and all we have to do is introduce them to each other to find this out. The extraordinary fact, which is repeated so constantly by people from Northern Ireland, is that neither side ever met a Protestant or a Catholic until they were twenty years of age and had either left the province or gone to university. Meeting people is the cure for xenophobia. Push them into each other's faces until they recognise consanguinity.

The early history of the European Union embodies this notion. Jean Monnet was the inspiration. Two peoples fresh from internecine warfare building a future together. How is it to be done? Two simple principles: enlightened self-interest and managed co-operation. Do not mention peace, and do not expect people to work for nothing: evacuate all volunteers.

After twenty years experience of what was euphemistically called 'the troubles' in the North, the time came for us to discover at least two things: there is no easy solution to this problem; and 90% of our people on both sides of the border accept that fact and want to live out their lives in peace harmony and prosperity. We needed a magic formula which would show us how to harness passion, how to attach it to our waning economy and make it profitable for all of us.

Thirty years before, the most strife-torn land mass on our planet, sown with more blood, hatred and bitterness than was known before in human history, decided to opt for constructiveness rather than destruction and the

European Union was born. It was not a united political entity, it was a fragile bond of continual dialogue, lasting sometimes into the exhausting hours of the late evening and early morning. But it worked and, more importantly, it healed wounds between Germans, Belgians, French, British, and nations that a few short years before found themselves in the cauldron of conflict. The 'entrepreneurial peace-maker' believes that such a transformation could work for the island of Ireland. The machinery is there, the funds are there, the expertise and the experience are there. We are the only ones who are not yet there.

The transformation of Ireland over the past thirty years serves as a testament to the workings of the 'entrepreneurial peace-maker'. The past thirty years have been witness to an economic revolution in Ireland with the advent of innovations such as Shannon Airport, Shannon town and Shannon Industrial Zone emerging from the disused area of an unlikely desert. Transformations such as these, on the small and the large scale, were the result of managed co-operation.

It is this ambition and energy which helped to transform Ireland which is needed to address the issue of peace in Northern Ireland. No pious speculation, no political promises. A hard-nosed realism and an investment for our children would get business people on both sides interested. Invest today in reconciliation and reap tomorrow economic stability, that is the message of the 'entrepreneurial peace-maker'. The cost of one day's violence was more than most businesses could afford to invest over ten years in their own future.

The idea is right and the structures are in place. The 'entrepreneurial peace-maker' was and is an inspiration to us to get our act together, not just to get on with our business and overcome whatever prevents us from living and working together, but to bottle the formula once it has been proven, and make it one of the most sought after products of the Celtic Tiger.

So, what are we waiting for, I say, let's get on with it.

The best way I know to defeat an enemy is to make him a friend.

Abraham Lincoln

An Iota of Peace

Edward Horgan

Edward Horgan is a researcher at the Centre for Peace and Development Studies at the University of Limerick. He served in the Irish Defence Forces for over twenty years, which included several tours of duty as a United Nations peacekeeper. He has a BA in History, Politics and Social Studies from the University of Limerick and an M.Phil. (Peace Studies) from the Irish School of Ecumenics, Trinity College, Dublin.

Following the crimes against humanity committed in the United States on 11th September 2001, it has become more difficult to focus coherent thoughts on issues of peace. Yet, it has never been more important, as leaders of nations, great and small, talk of war and crusades. They admonish dissenting voices that anyone who does not agree with the reaction of the US led alliance, to what is called the threat of Islamic terrorism, is against the civilization and democracy of the Western World and, by default, is supporting terrorism. Like the script of an old-fashioned black and white Western movie, the good guys must get the bad guys *"dead or alive"*.

Human interaction, whether at individual or global level, is seldom so clear-cut. In this globalised world of complex interdependency, peace, security and justice cannot be achieved in isolation from each other, or exclusively for one group, at the expense of others. The idea is being promoted that it is Western civilization and democracy that is under attack and must be defended. This presupposes the superiority of Western society, ignoring such aberrations as the Holocaust, the Vietnam War, the depravation caused and still being caused by slavery and colonialism, as well as incidents of state orchestrated terrorism. Yet listing the crimes of history tends only to inflame and to blame and will not resolve the critical issues facing the world today, just as they will not be resolved by inappropriate military responses to terrorism.

Now is not the time for knee-jerk reactions and condemnations, or for simplistic solutions to complex problems. The issues involved are far too serious. In this age of proliferation of weapons of mass destruction, world leaders do not have the luxury of learning from their own mistakes. It is now, as never before, imperative to resolve conflict between nations and between peoples, and to get it right, first time. A terrorist attack, or an industrial accident at the Sellafield nuclear complex, could leave large areas of Europe polluted with radiation for generations. Such an assault on the environment is an assault on humanity, whether committed by evil men, or careless industrialists. Such a scenario is just one, and not the most catastrophic possibility if global crisis management fails on this occasion. The right of countries such as the United States to defend its citizens is not in dispute. Defending innocent people is not just a right of governments, it is a duty, but it does not just apply to innocent people in Western society, it applies equally to all humanity.

I have witnessed the pain and injustices perpetrated on all three communities in central Bosnia and in Vukovar, Croatia, where I served as a United Nations Volunteer during 1996. Over seven thousand Muslim men were murdered in Srebrenica in 1995 while the world looked on and some United Nations peacekeepers stood helplessly by. In the Northern Ireland conflict, in the Balkans and in World War Two, history has been manipulated by terrorist individuals and groups and by some states, to achieve their own objectives at the expense of many innocent victims. As with the Jewish Holocaust in World War Two, it is already too late to be seeking justice for the victims who have been murdered in such conflicts. The only worthwhile atonement that can be achieved on their behalf is the establishment of global peace and justice. The Jewish people are entitled, more than most others, to a homeland and to peace. Yet, imposing a solution to the Jewish problem at the expense of the Palestinian people, is the equivalent of punishing the Palestinian people for the horrific crimes of World War Two in which Palestinians played no part.

In Cambodia, a murderous autogenocide was perpetrated in a country destabilised by the US/Vietnam war while the international community again stood idly by. In Rwanda in 1994, and in much of Central and Western Africa in the meantime, millions of innocent people have died, directly as a result of local wars and genocide, but indirectly resulting from colonialism and neo-colonialism and exploitation. In Zimbabwe I witnessed a two year-old African boy who had been beaten because his father was an opposition supporter and worked as a farm labourer on a farm owned by a person of European origin. This crime was committed in the name of justice and equality for black Africans. While this problem has colonial roots, its more immediate causes are local abuse of power and corruption. Such cases demonstrate the complexities of injustices resulting from modern conflicts and should signal caution against simplistic solutions to complex problems. In many African conflicts, the so-called Western 'civilized' world is still standing idly by, except for inappropriate intervention in Somalia and inadequate and seriously inappropriate intervention in Rwanda.

Such arguments in no way excuse the crimes committed in the USA on 11th September. Each such crime against humanity has its own unique set of immediate causes but most have interconnected root causes. Identifying these root causes is probably the most important task facing those promoting the cause of peace. The elimination of these root causes is likely to be the peace-makers' most difficult, but most important, task. While the Palestine/Israeli conflict is but one of the issues behind the current crisis, and is being cynically manipulated by the terrorists leaders, a just resolution to this conflict, which has continued for over two generations, must be achieved before the threats of further terrorist attacks will recede. I witnessed the aftermath of the Yom Kippur war as an Irish military peace-keeper in 1973. I was impressed both by the futility of the war itself and the suffering and deaths it caused and by the relative success of the UNEF II peacekeeping mission which helped to restore some peace between Israel and Egypt. The role of peacekeeper is not an easy one, as is testified to by the long roll of honour of those Irish soldiers who have given their lives in the cause of peace.

More recently, I have witnessed the efforts of many dedicated individuals and organisations while working on election missions and democratisation programmes in the Balkans, Nigeria, Indonesia, Zimbabwe and East Timor. In many cases the progress is slow and the contribution of each individual may seem tiny. However, it is such small contributions that add up to real progress towards global peace and justice. Each *iota* of such success towards peace is far more powerful than the most sophisticated Cruise missile. The dogs of war bark loudly, while the doves of peace work quietly. However, the massive power unleashed by war leads only to destruction and sows the seeds of further terrorism. Let us hope that the multiple *iotas* of effort towards peace with justice, like tiny mustard seed in the desert of conflict, can blossom forth into an oasis of hope for the future of humankind.

Civilizations should be measured by the degree of diversity
attained and the degree of unity retained.

W.H. Auden

Peace is a Cliché

Christopher Hudson

Christopher Hudson received an MBE in 1999 for his work on the Peace Train and the peace process in Northern Ireland. He is also Honorary Chair of Oxfam Ireland. Chris is Organising Officer for the Communication Workers' Union, Ireland, and has been involved in organising many delivery companies and call centres. He was also involved in the production of the E-work Forum's Code of Practice on Teleworking on behalf of the Irish Congress of Trade Unions, and is involved in n a number of European projects such as Telmet and Tosca.

Recently I was discussing theatre with a number of my friends and what they had seen and what they hoped to see in the forthcoming Dublin Theatre Festival. We got onto a discussion about various playwrights and their merits and creditability. I asked one friend if he had ever attended a Shakespearean play and he informed me yes he had, he went to see Hamlet but, like all Shakespearean plays, it was full of clichés.

Although this was said in a humorous manner it set me thinking about the peace industry, which probably has more clichés than any Shakespearean play. If I hear once again that much abused line from William Butler Yeats "peace comes dropping slowly" I will crack up. Sometimes the use of language associated with the peace industry can not only be offensive but can actually be provocative. How often have we heard that those who voted "no" against the Good Friday or Belfast Agreement are against peace? On RTE there is a regular mantra with various people, in particular from the Nationalist community, when they are being interviewed, discussing any criticism of their respective positions, that those who are criticising them are against the peace process. Peace should not be another weapon in the armoury of either side to bash what we commonly call 'the other side' over the head. I wonder should we even use the word peace in our deliberations, but instead try to manage our language without the biggest cliché of them all.

I have always regarded my involvement with Northern Ireland as a journey of understanding. What do I mean by that? Well I come from a Republican Nationalist background with a strong tradition and family involvement in the Republican movement in the early part of the 20th century. Indeed my family can claim one martyr, Joseph Hudson, who died in the Civil War, killed by free state troops. There is a road called after him, Hudson Road, in the borough of Dun Laoire. As a young man my passion for all things Republican could not be exceeded and when the troubles broke out in Northern Ireland I shared with most people in the South a view that our people, i.e. Catholic Nationalists, were being set upon and slaughtered and discriminated against by the other side i.e. Protestant Unionists.

It was black and white and did not need any clarification, we all knew which was the right side and which was the wrong side. We all knew the universal comparisons, South Africa and apartheid, the Negroes in America, hence the song 'We shall overcome'. However the last thirty odd years have been a journey for me just like everybody else and as I began to learn about 'the other side' I could see many aspects of the integrity of their argument which rang true. They were a minority on this island, the only way to protect themselves was to retain the link with the United Kingdom and retain a state within the United Kingdom that gave them protection.

I now believe that a united Ireland would not serve the Unionist community well. Why do I say this? I do not believe that Nationalist Ireland would be generous in a united Ireland to Ulster Protestant Unionists. The evidence is there. The exodus from Derry of Protestant people and the refusal to recognise Protestant West Belfast. Also in the Republic of Ireland where Nationalism is confident, strong in its belief in itself, and indeed the country is performing economically and culturally better than most other countries in Europe, there is still no real generous outpouring to the Unionist community. Essentially they are treated with contempt and one has only to notice the different tones when Peter Robinson is being interviewed by RTE in comparison to when Séamus Mallon is being interviewed. Orangemen, that is Dublin and Wicklow Orangemen, are afraid to hold a traditional march in Dublin, yet they are citizens of the Irish Republic. Not only that, but orange is included in our National flag which recognises them allegedly as equals. Only in Rosnowlagh in Donegal is there a traditional Orange march in the whole of the Republic of Ireland. This does not bode well for our recent immigrants who will eventually become part of the tapestry that is Irish life. By that I mean Orthodox Romanians and Islamic communities from Nigeria and other African states. Will they get short shift? Will they be allowed to celebrate national feast days, cultural traditions and public manifestations of their religion and culture?

There is a real need to fully understand pluralism and diversity in the Republic of Ireland. I do not believe we have arrived at that situation as yet. We are not an inclusive society. There is a comfortable feeling about Irish Nationalism that makes others feel excluded. It may be the sounds of a GAA game on the radio on a Sunday that to many is exciting and the essence of being Irish, but yet to others is intimidating and frightening.

But time is on our side and we can begin to understand each other in a complete way and not in some superficial concept of building peace. We can become completely pluralist and inclusive. I believe it is time for serious dialogue between the GAA and the Orange Order with no intermediaries, no facilitators, but the Orange Order and the GAA talking to each other directly. It is time for those like the Taoiseach and the Attorney General, Michael McDowell, when they state they are in favour of a united Ireland to spell out what does that mean. How would they see the Gardai fitting into that united Ireland? How would they see the South making dramatic changes in every aspect of its life to include a million people who are absolutely hostile to any concept of living in a united Ireland? But, more importantly, talk about a united Ireland could be better left on the back burner and instead concentrate on a process of learning with regard to the other community, a process which involves a full understanding by the Nationalist tradition of the Protestant Ulster Orange tradition and *visa versa*. Understanding why a Loyalist would say to me "they love a token Prod on the Falls Road but we have no need for token Catholics on the Shankill". We, and by we I mean those of us from the Catholic Nationalist tradition, have to begin to understand why someone would make such a statement. Let us start that journey by entering into real dialogue which can take us on a journey to a place we never imagined we would visit. This place would not be a united Ireland as expressed by most Republicans and Nationalists, but a far more interesting Ireland, a far more inclusive, pluralistic, culturally diverse and dare I say it, peaceful Ireland. Then I will begin to feel proud to be Irish.

When evil men plot, good men must plan. When evil men burn and bomb, good men must build and bind. When evil men shout ugly words of hatred, good men must commit themselves to the glories of love.

Dr. Martin Luther King Jr.

Peace On The Ground Needs Support

Tony Kennedy

Tony Kennedy has served as Chief Executive of Co-operation Ireland since 1992. He holds a BSc (Hons) in Social Services and Technology from Loughborough University and an MSc in Public Policy, Planning and Administration from the University of Ulster. Previously he was Chief Housing Officer, Wakefield MDC, Regional Director (NW) of the Northern Ireland Housing Executive and Area Housing Manager, Belfast N.I. Housing Executive. He is involved in numerous associations and is a member of the Institute for Multi-Track Diplomacy, Civitas and the Association of European Border Regions. He is also the Deputy Director of the Ulidia Housing Association and the John Hewitt International Summer School. Tony also serves as the Chairman of the Irish Platform for Peace and Reconciliation.

While governments and the media concentrate on the political and military aspects of the peace process, the vital work of peace building at a community level needs to be properly recognised and supported.

Over three years after the signing of the Peace Agreement, at the end of July 2001, a young Protestant man - Gavin Brett - was shot by (it is believed) the Ulster Defence Association, going under the cover name of the Red Hand Commandos. His killers thought he was a Catholic, but the mistake won't matter to them - a 'bad Prod' (i.e. one talking to friends outside a GAA pitch) is considered as much a target as a Catholic. His murder brought the number of people killed by paramilitary organisations in Northern Ireland and the Republic of Ireland from the signing of the Agreement to around ninety.

From the ceasefires in 1994 to July 2001 at least 2,600 people were expelled from their homes in Northern Ireland. All paramilitary organisations were involved; sometimes paramilitary rivalries within each community caused as much distress as those between republican and loyalist groups. The summer of 2001 saw the highest level of street violence for many years, particularly in the old battle grounds of North Belfast where attacks and counter attacks have been made on houses and community centres and halls on either side of the 'peace lines'. Churches and halls associated with cultural activities were favourite targets. Whatever exists, it certainly wasn't peace.

We will have peace only when we have created societies where people feel secure with their identity and, as a result, are secure enough to seek to understand and respect the identities of others, and to permit others to express their cultural traditions as they see fit.

From its very beginning there has been a flaw in the peace process. It concentrated almost solely on the political and the military (or paramilitary) processes without addressing the core issue of relationships between people. Building peace has become the preserve of the governments and the political parties without any significant involvement from others.

This attitude is hardly new. Contrast humanity's attitudes to war and to peace on the island of Ireland and elsewhere. When a declaration of war is issued, we accept that we must devote all the efforts of society to winning the war. When a declaration of peace is signed, it is assumed that war is over and that collective efforts can cease. In reality the task of building peace is more important and more difficult than waging war, and demands greater, rather than less, resources and effort.

In the years since the ceasefires of 1994, endless hours have been devoted to sorting out the political and the military aspects of the process. Assistance has been sought and received from the United States, Canada, South Africa and Finland. No such similar effort and resource has been put into peace building.

There has of course been some support for community peace building from the European Union through the Special Support Programmes for Peace and Reconciliation but, in the absence of a clear policy framework, much of this support has been dissipated. It is right for example that issues of social exclusion and economic development should be addressed as part of a peace process. But addressing these issues without reference to the core issues of addressing diverse identities and reconciling divided communities is missing the point. If real peace is to be achieved, the Irish Government and the Northern Ireland administration must make peace building at a community level a core policy priority in government plans.

The partnership approach which has been successful in promoting economic development should be extended to peace building, and reconciliation organisations should be welcomed as social partners and encouraged to assist in policy development. Within a clear policy framework, government departments and other public agencies should be required to produce action plans to promote inter-community understanding and respect, and publish targets for the achievement of these plans.

The Co-operation Ireland survey on attitudes, undertaken in the summer of 2001, showed how much work still needs to be done. It showed that levels of understanding in the Republic for both communities in Northern Ireland were very low. Only 28% of people in the Republic felt that they had a good or excellent understanding of the protestant tradition in Northern Ireland. Only 36% felt they similarly understood the catholic/nationalist tradition. Understanding in Northern Ireland wasn't much better. Only 19% of Protestants in Northern Ireland surveyed claimed that they had a good or excellent understanding of the culture and traditions of the Republic.

The survey also showed an alarming number of people not only don't know but also don't care for the cultures of others. 40% of people in the Republic were not interested in learning more about the protestant/unionist tradition and 68% of Protestants in Northern Ireland weren't interested in learning more about the Republic. Regrettably, this relative ignorance and lack of interest in learning more doesn't stop people having an opinion of others, usually hostile.

At the same time there is a substantial group which wants to get to know about different cultures on the island, but doesn't have the opportunity. Research into conflict resolution locally and internationally has shown that long term sustained co-operation on issues of common concern is one of the few approaches known to work in promoting reconciliation in divided societies. This co-operation must be assisted and managed, reassuring and supporting those involved.

It is right and important that the governments and political parties devote substantial efforts to resolving political difficulties. This is an essential prerequisite to building peace. However, it will never be sufficient in itself.

If we are to build peace, we require the same level of commitment to community peace building as is devoted to political and security issues. Our political leaders must dedicate themselves to improving inter-community and north/south relationships in real partnership with all sectors of society. Too much time has been lost already. The time to start is now.

Since wars begin in the minds of men,
it is in the minds of men that the
defenses of peace must be constructed

Constitution of UNESCO, 1945

The Voice of Peace
Brendan Kennelly

Brendan Kennelly was educated at St Ita's College, Tarbert, County Kerry, TCD and Leeds University. He has lectured in English literature in TCD from 1963 to date, became Associate Professor of Modern Literature in 1969 and professor in 1973. He has lectured in US colleges and was Gildersleeve Professor of Literature at Barnard College, New York in 1971 and taught in Pennsylvania 1971–2. He is the recipient of the AE Memorial Prize for Poetry 1967 and Critics' Special Harvey Award 1988.

I am
Beyond all things
Even in your dream

Of me.
I am farther than
The last syllable of the

Last poem.
It is so still
Where I am

That the infant's breath
Is monstrous
And death itself

Is a swilling pig
In a sty of silence.
Here

I quiet the boisterous stars.
Obliterate
All thought of war

While my influence
Breathes in the dog's throat
And the moulded stones

Of the sea that wait
For the bully's hand
To hurl his hate

Through the night
Of smashed families
You soon forget

Yet I exist for him, for you.
What you wish, I am.
You speak of me

But do not accept me.
Let me be more to you
Then a vague wish,

An excuse to kill.
I will change if you let me
I will.

Promoting Religious Tolerance
Maryam Kiely

Maryam Kiely is a third year student at the University of Limerick.

"Among the basic human rights, the right to follow ones conscience in matters of religion and belief is undoubtedly the most cherished, so much so that people have been willing to endure the severest trials and even to lay down their lives rather than to surrender this fundamental right. And yet throughout history this human right has been frequently and openly violated. Strange indeed that the violators are most often those who consider themselves faithful followers of a religion".

The Bahá'i International Community submitted this excerpt, taken from a statement entitled *Promoting Religious Tolerance*, to the United Nations Commission on Human Rights. It describes a particular violation of human rights that has existed since the beginning of time throughout the world. Those of us living on the North Atlantic island of Ireland can strongly empathise with this statement as in some ways it depicts what for us has been a reality for hundreds of years.

When we consider the thirty years of conflict and the 3,500 lives that were lost during 'The Troubles' in Northern Ireland it may seem relatively simple to blame it on religious intolerance, politics breaking down or just plain history. However, to do this would be to ignore the principal and underlying problem, which is lack of unity. Bahá'u'lláh, Founder of the Bahá'i Faith, said: *"the well being of mankind, its peace and security are unattainable unless and until its unity is firmly established"*. One can hardly dispute the fact that Northern Ireland is a much-divided place, which has suffered atrocities on both sides of the political divide. Before we can attempt to achieve any form of peace, unity must first be established in the Northern community. Let us now examine the infamous Good Friday Agreement and assess the impact it has had on the people of Northern Ireland.

"Raw emotion, joy, wonder and disbelief swirled around Castle Buildings yesterday. And when the light of dawn broke it chased away the political darkness of Northern Ireland to reveal a promise that things could be different", wrote Frank Millar, London Editor of *The Irish Times*. Perhaps he spoke too soon. The world at large rejoiced, when on April 10th, 1998, after twenty-one months of negotiations, agreement had finally been reached. All appeared to be going well on May 22nd when over 71% in the North, almost 95% in the Republic, voted 'yes' in the Referendum thereby giving their support to the hard won Agreement. Further encouragement and recognition was given on October 16th when John Hume and David Trimble were awarded the 1998 Nobel Peace Prize for *"their efforts to find a peaceful solution to the conflict in Northern Ireland"*. Although Trimble, leader of the Ulster Unionist Party and the First Minister of Northern Ireland, said that the award was a great honour he sounded a note of caution by adding that he hoped the Nobel Committee had not been *"premature"*.

Now almost two years since the signing of the Agreement, we have been forced to accept the harsh reality that despite the efforts made on all sides, the Agreement has failed to establish a peaceful Northern Ireland. Since the signing of the Agreement 114 people in the North have died as a result of ongoing terrorist attacks *(The Guardian)*. Disputes over Orange Order parades, rows over punishment beatings, the Omagh bombing and the decommissioning deadlock did nothing to help the fragile Peace Process. The final and most recent blow came on Friday the 11th of February 2001 when the Secretary of State for Northern Ireland, Peter Mandelson M.P. temporarily suspended the institutions set up under the Agreement. In the lull that has ensued we may well ask: are we just going round in circles? Why is the path to peace so fraught with complications? Is the state of peace that the Agreement sought to establish a possibility?

Allow me to return to the previously mentioned concept of unity. Many people speak of a United Ireland but the real issue is creating a united Northern Ireland. Only when the people of the North can put aside their differences and agree to compromise for the greater good, will the peace process take on any real meaning. The task of undoing years of violence and prejudice is far from easy but let us not lose heart, progress, albeit slow and difficult, has been made and I am confident that Northern Ireland can have a bright future.

> *"Perhaps as much effort needs to be expended in the education of all persons on this planet, from the earliest age... and certainly with a strong focus on the most malleable and impressionable stages of human existence... on long-range steps to achieve a lasting peace, and provide for a society in which human happiness can flourish for everyone". (Bahá'í International Community)*

The highest result of education is tolerance.

Helen Keller

A Cold House

Gordon Lucy

Gordon Lucy is the Director of the Ulster Society, a cultural organisation with the remit of promoting Ulster - British Heritage and Culture. He is also a member of the Northern Ireland Civic Forum, serving on the cultural panel.

The United Kingdom strives to be a genuinely plural, multi-national, multi-cultural state capable of accommodating diversity and difference. The British state accommodates two distinct systems of law, three of education, two established churches, different languages and many distinctive traditions. More than a century ago the liberal Catholic historian Lord Acton justly contended that human welfare was best served in a plural and multi-national state, a view to which the great Canadian statesman Pierre Trudeau passionately subscribed in more recent times.

As a unionist, one is obliged to regret the secession of the twenty-six counties from the United Kingdom that sundered the unity of the British archipelago. One is also obliged to note that the twenty-six county state has been a conspicuously less plural society than the United Kingdom, not surprisingly, because the principal impulse to repeal, home rule and, ultimately, separatism was not pluralist. Daniel O' Connell campaigned for repeal because he believed that overwhelmingly Roman Catholic Ireland should not be governed by the predominantly Protestant Parliament of the United Kingdom. Although Isaac Butt and C.S. Parnell were both Protestants, the vast majority of those who sought home rule between the

1870s and the outbreak of the Great War almost certainly would have empathised with O' Connell's case for repeal.

When the twenty-six counties achieved 'native government' in the early 1920s the new political elite, 'cradle Catholics' virtually to a man and products of the Gaelic League, consciously sought to create a state that was Catholic and Gaelic. If the latter was to prove rather more daunting than anticipated, the former was more readily accomplished. The failure of Dr. Garret Fitzgerald's 'constitutional crusade' launched in 1981, the Roman Catholic hierarchy's blunt assertion to the New Ireland Forum in 1984 that "The rights of the minority are no more sacred than the rights of the majority", and the outcome of the referenda on abortion and divorce in 1983 and 1986 respectively; all demonstrate that until comparatively recently pluralism had at best a modest place in the scheme of things in the Republic. Little wonder that the journalist Stanley Gebler Davies sought to explain the Irish Republic to an English readership by observing that the Republic was not so much a foreign country as a Catholic one.

In his acceptance speech at the Nobel Prize award ceremony in Oslo in December 1999 David Trimble conceded that Ulster Unionists had "built a solid house but it was a cold house for Catholics". People in the twenty-six county state appreciate insufficiently the extent to which they created a cold house for Protestants. Whereas the minority community in Northern Ireland has increased in both percentage and absolute terms, the fate of the minority in the twenty-six county state has been in remorseless decline in both percentage and absolute terms. Indeed, the historian Theodore Hoppen has observed:

> *The tragedy of southern Protestantism lies in the fact that, by the time it had developed enough confidence to accept changed circumstances, it had virtually ceased to exist.*

Since the 1990s, for a variety of reasons, the Republic has become a more plural society, a welcome development. There is a relationship between that pluralism and the phenomenon of the 'Celtic Tiger'. Pluralism produces better economic performance than autarky.

Pluralism is not always easy as the recent debates in both the United Kingdom and the Republic about refugees and asylum seekers reveal but, as Richard Morrison pointed out in The Times (21 June 2001) during 'Refugee Week', persecuted foreigners have created much of what we accept as the very essence of British culture - from fish and chips (a Huguenot dish), and Handel's Messiah (and here Dubliners may smile) to ITV, Marks and Spencer...and chicken tikka masala. As, generally speaking, the Irish diaspora was welcomed around the world and has prospered; the attitude towards immigrants by some Irish people is profoundly disappointing. But then so too is the attitude of some British people.

There is never room for complacency. Hailing the apparent triumph of liberal democracy and capitalism, in 1992 Francis Fukuyama confidently predicted 'the end of history' but failed to anticipate the resurgence of ethnic nationalism around the world. Unfortunately, Samuel Huntington, the author of *The Clash of Civilisations and the Remaking of the World Order* (1993), offered a more realistic guide to the future when he observed:

> *In the post-Cold War World the most important distinctions are not ideological, political or economic. they are cultural. People are attempting to answer the most basic questions humans can face: who are we?*

That question can be answered in both a benign and a malign way. Ethnic nationalism's answer is invariably malign and the antithesis of pluralism. In the recent United Kingdom general election Sinn Féin described its electoral gains as the 'greening of the west', terminology redolent of Sinn Féin/IRA's 'ethnic cleansing' of previous decades. Sinn Féin as a party exerts an increasingly malign influence on the politics of Northern Ireland but as a result of 'low standards in high places' Sinn Féin seems to be poised on the brink of exerting a pivotal role in, and equally malign influence on, the politics of the Republic. It is a truly sad commentary on the state of public life in the Republic that murderers and their apologists can appear to be high-minded idealists, especially to the young.

Stephen I, the 11th century founder of a strong and independent Hungarian state and its first king, clearly was an intelligent ruler and an exponent of pluralism when he observed:

> *A kingdom of one language and one way of life would be weak and fragile…Foreigners should be welcomed: their different languages and customs, their example and their arms, would…enrich the kingdom and deter its enemies.*

Some societies - Athens in the Age of Pericles, the 17th century Dutch Republic and the United Kingdom - have embraced the plural vision; others - Sparta, Louise XIV's France and Ireland until very recently - have not, preferring a monist vision for society. History and experience suggest that plural societies are invariably more successful societies. They are also much more interesting societies in which to live. Intelligent people recognise the inevitability and the value of diversity. Society, like cloth is more attractive when woven from different strands. Plural societies are happier societies. People should welcome, enjoy and celebrate diversity.

Never look down on anybody unless you're helping him up.

Jesse Jackson

Channels of Peace?

Roy Magee

Reverend Dr. Roy Magee is a Presbyterian minister based in East Belfast, a stronghold of the most active loyalist paramilitary groups in Northern Ireland. He has worked tirelessly to move the paramilitary organisations away from violence and to point them toward a democratic peaceful resolution. For this ongoing work, he is largely responsible for having brokered the loyalist cease-fire which was announced in October 1994.

Those of us who are old enough and unfortunate enough to have experienced the hideous atrocities of conflict do not want ever again to live through such degrading and often dehumanising events. However, while the vast majority of people want peace, they invariably see it as the responsibility of others to deliver. It is important to realise that while in Northern Ireland there were, and unfortunately still are, terrorists who must stand condemned, each one of us played a part in creating the climate in which violence was bred, nurtured and nourished. Therefore before we can move forward constructively, there needs to be an acknowledgement that individually each of us has a vital part to play and we must make a conscious decision to work positively towards that end. This demands, amongst other things:

1) Looking at each situation from the other person's point of view.
2) Seeking to satisfy the other person's needs and address his fears.
3) Striving always to have a *positive* rather than a *negative* attitude towards others.
4) Training ourselves to *hear* what those from whom we differ are saying. This is essential for the simple reason that if we fail to *hear* a person, we are sending a signal that we don't *respect* him.
5) Putting others first. In an age in which everyone is demanding his own rights, such an attitude is not popular.

6) Acknowledging our mistakes. Such a step is difficult in a terrorist culture because the terrorist of whatever hue perceives an admission of wrong-doing as not only betraying his *cause*, but also condemning the actions of his colleagues who, after all, are merely soldiers fighting for what they hold dear.

7) Taking positive steps towards *reconciliation*. Because this involves confession and a desire for forgiveness, it is undoubtedly the most difficult part of a *peace process*. If, however, meaningful and lasting relationships are to take place, happen it must. Let me hasten to add that *reconciliation* is the most advanced stage and would normally come much further along the road. Moving towards *reconciliation* involves striving to achieve basic values such as (i) human dignity, (ii) equality - this involves the abolition of sectarianism, (iii) justice (iv) freedom - not to do what I want (that's licence) but freedom from being forced to do what others want me to do, (v) right to life.

8) Working constructively to rid ourselves of *hatred*. Often because of the community into which we have been born, the circumstances in which we have grown up, the companions with which we have been surrounded or the clichés we unquestioningly accepted, we imagine those who are of a different religious persuasion or political affiliation as trying to undermine both our faith and nationality and therefore a threat. Because we have expended all our energy in building walls to keep us apart rather than bridges over which we can cross to get closer to each other, we despise not only what we imagine the perceived enemy is trying to do, but we also despise who he is. So we *insult* him, *shame* him, *ridicule* him and believe *unconfirmed* stories against him, with the result that very soon we HATE him and everyone like him. If untreated, our *hate* soon turns to *rage* and we become *addicts who mainline on bigotry* and *bitterness..*

When the cease-fires were announced, many people expected to find, if not the following day, certainly very soon, all violence ended and perhaps even weapons decommissioned. Unfortunately, since we are the products of our history, community and homes, it would be unlikely to find what has been in place for hundreds of years changed overnight. Peace in Ireland, almost of necessity, will be a gradual, painful process which will come about through interaction, a willingness to forgive and a patient building of trust. It is a road that will be littered with pitfalls, obstacles and disappointments.

T.D. Jakes relates how, as a boy, when his mother was baking he used to enjoy scraping the bowl, always ending up with his face covered with batter. Years later he realised that this must be his philosophy for life *viz "If you want to enjoy life to the fullest possible, don't wait for what's in the oven, take the bowl now and get something out of every part".* Too many of us spend our lives waiting for the 'main event' and miss the benefits and blessings of the period in which we are living. We need to take time to enjoy where we are on the way to where we are going. *Peace* is not the property of any particular group - it belongs to *all* and governments must ensure that no minority, however vicious or heavily armed, is allowed to deprive us of it. As the Prince of Peace Himself stated in what we refer to as the Sermon on the Mount, *"Peace does not just happen it is made"* and that requires unbroken effort. Indeed the word which is translated *'peacemaker'* was used in classical Greek for ambassadors who were commissioned to negotiate peace between alienated parties - a task which demanded enterprise and effort. In a reference to this beatitude *"Blessed are the peacemakers"*, John Blanchard, the Bible teacher and Author says, *"United States President, Abraham Lincoln once wrote, 'Die when I may I would like it to be said that I always pulled up a weed and planted a flower where I thought a flower would grow'."* While this is hardly an adequate expression of what is meant by this beatitude, it nevertheless helps us to realise that *peacemaking* requires effort. As the Apostle Paul commands in his Epistle to the Romans *"make every effort to live in peace with all men".* It is difficult to overcome our prejudices, to suppress our natural feelings or even at times to yield ground over an issue in which no principle is involved. Haven't many of us discovered from experience it is exceedingly hard work to have a peaceable relationship with those who are fundamentally different from us or whose religion, culture, ethnic identity and nationality are not the same as ours? However this may be, we have a bounden duty to 'make every effort' - it is *not* an optional extra.

Perhaps in the midst of what many see as a shaky situation, the Northern Ireland Assembly, supported by the British and Irish Governments, should declare a specific day as a *Peace Day*.

It could be a day in which *Church leaders, politicians, paramilitaries, loyal orders, residents groups, businessmen*, and indeed *people in all walks of life* would sign publicly a commitment along the following lines:

1) We unreservedly pledge ourselves to endeavour to find a solution to our problems only by *peaceful, democratic* and *lawful* means.
2) Realising that *life* and *death* are in the power of the tongue, we promise to exercise extreme care in all language we use and in particular when called upon to make public utterances.
3) Acknowledging that *human life* is *sacrosanct* and that injuring another human being is contrary to the will of God, we commit ourselves to do all in our power to prevent the injury of our fellows of whatever creed or political persuasion.

Yes, the *peace* may be fragile but surely what we have is light-years better than what we had pre-ceasefires and it is vital that every man, woman and young person recognise his or her responsibility to water and feed the tender plant so that it will flourish and bring forth an abundance of fruit.

Peace is not Pax Romana
John Mathers

*John Mathers is a farmer for many years after various jobs and
ventures abroad. He is an arts graduate and takes a keen interest in
politics.*

Imperial Rome managed to bring about a low level of violence and it
was known as Pax Romana. It was an armed peace as brute force was
used to cow the people down. Crime was low for the wrong reason; fear of
terrible retribution. Power was delegated to a local strongman that ran the
area, collected the taxes and paid some to Rome. Strong-arm tactics kept
the peace rather than education fostering brotherly love and respect for the
law. The present peace process has not got rid of the paramilitaries,
punishment beatings and expulsions. It has increased polarisation, polluted
our democracy and there is a danger that we will have a version of Pax
Romana and not real peace. A contaminated environment is where we
must befriend thugs to protect us from other thugs. When paramilitaries
control the street then protection money or membership of a group is
necessary to survive. The streetwise close their eyes and keep their mouths
shut except to shout slogans and throw stones across the divide on cue.

Real peace needs a change in education and the social environment. Brecht
said unhappy is the land that needs heroes. Worse still, when the media
glamorises or makes martyrs out of monsters. Sick too, is the society that
looks on suicide as an heroic act. Those heroes said things like; no
compromise, we will wade through rivers of blood to achieve our aims or, it
is good to warm the cold earth with the red blood of young men.

141

Monuments are erected to them in many places, even inside churches. In World War One the bang-bang nationalist sided with Germany rather than the democracies. The Kaiser was a demigod; ruled by decree and ignored humanitarian codes. In World War Two the same blinkered mindset opted for neutrality while the democracies were fighting gangster regimes perpetrating the most evil crimes that ever occurred in the world. We must stop tribal reckoning in deciding what cause to support and use a humanitarian yardstick. Relations with others should depend on the others having a good human rights record.

There is an old story of two Clonmacnoise monks returning from the west. At a crossing point on the Shannon just south of Clonmacnoise they met a young woman. The woman was afraid to wade across the river, as the water was higher and the current faster than she expected. She asked the monks to carry her across. The old monk said we are not allowed to touch a woman. The young monk was moved by pity for her plight and he put her on his shoulders and carried her across. The old monk ran to the monastery and reported the misdemeanour of his young colleague. When the young monk arrived at the monastery he found the gate locked and a very angry Abbot. The Abbot said *"you broke the rules by having a woman on your shoulders and you are now expelled."* The young monk departed but not before saying *"I had a woman on my shoulders for five minutes but it seems to me that you have a woman on your shoulders twenty four hours a day, every day of your life".* Like the Abbot we have goblins of history on our backs and like all baggage it hinders us in relating to strangers or settling down in foreign places. We should remember our humanity and forget the rest, especially our slanted version of history, adopt a culture that fits us and helps us to prosper in a global village. A revenge culture and beggar your neighbour policies will not accelerate our progress in a global market.

Academic freedom will help people to mix and dispel myths. People should be encouraged to have enquiring minds, to make their own contacts across the divide, gather their own facts and be encouraged to reach their own conclusions. A lot of violence is caused by leaders lying to us or our parents lying to us and we readily accepting the stereotype that is passed down to us. In the same way pragmatism and reason help to look again at the problem, search for a new solution, rather than rub salt into old wounds. To be humble and not to be dogmatic, to compromise and to realise that sub-optimisation, is the basis of all good working relationships.

Real peace is based on humanitarian values that are seen not just as of moral importance, but also a good investment as a prosperous community develops. The Ten Commandments are a sound economic code. The goal of government would be to promote economic welfare and human happiness through a good rounded education. Peace is part of the good man that loves his neighbour and, in order to do that, he must love himself and develop himself, so that he can render a service to his family and community. We should erect monuments to artists, musicians, inventors that increased the merry index and not the misery index. We are noted for the 'craic' and that merriment comes out of musical instruments and drinking glasses. There is more friendship in a pint of Guinness than a churn of buttermilk. Misery comes out of a gun. The 'craic' is a feast of music and a pouring of souls that lifts the spirits. Irish pubs with the diddly dee music are conquering the world. Peace is to win people over to you by offering a better quality life, sold with silky words. Take the challenge of Edward Carson, father of Unionism, seriously when he said in 1914, *"I say to my Nationalist fellow countrymen you have never tried to win over Ulster, showing that good government can come under the Home Rule Bill, try and win her over to the rest of Ireland. You probably can coerce her – though I doubt it. If you do, that will be disastrous for Ulster and the whole country".* Peace comes from a system where there is social mobility upwards for most people, where people reach their potential and the economic system provides opportunities for diverse talents and all the people. To have a good set of universal values; tolerance, understanding and all the values that help us to live and flourish in an open society. Such societies are attractive to outsiders. To encourage people to take personal responsibility and not blame the system, or as in history, blame the British for everything. A people that do not relish a challenge or face down a dangerous bully will end in poverty and disgrace and will find that the danger avoided has now multiplied.

Tribalism is an old problem and persists despite the Christian message of universal brotherhood and the DNA code telling us there is only one race; humanity. There is only one fatherland; the earth. In Jesus' time the Jews avoided the Samaritans. They would not enter the house of a Samaritan or use any instruments used by them. On the way to Galilee the Jews had to cross over the river Jordan and back again rather than go through the territory of Samaria. It reminds me of the ghettoised areas of Northern Ireland and a new version of the story the 'Good Samaritan'. A man fell among paramilitaries and he was beaten up and left in a bad state. Two politicians came along and looked at the injured man. They decided to ring for an ambulance, then to hurry to catch up with the people who committed the crime and find out what they want. *"We will give them what they want and they will cease such violence"* they said.

But smiting hands shall learn to heal,
To build as to destroy;
Nor less my heart for others feel
That I the more enjoy.

And so the shadows fall apart,
And so the west-winds play;
And all the windows of my heart
I open to the day.

John Greenleaf Whittier

Peace comes dropping slow...
Alf McCreary

Alf McCreary is an award-winning journalist and author who lives and works in Northern Ireland.

When I began writing about peace-making some thirty years ago, and trying to facilitate peace at a local level, I never dreamed that it would be so difficult or take so long. Now that I am older and hopefully a little wiser, I realise that it may take at least another generation for permanent peace to become a reality - but at least we are on the right track.

In my first weeks of journalism with the Belfast Telegraph I witnessed Ian Paisley and his followers throw snowballs in fury at the car of the Taioseach Sean Lemass as he left Stormont, having met the Unionist leader Terence O'Neill in what was then a brave, but doomed, attempt at peace-making across the border.

Within a short time I had a ringside seat as we watched the Northern Ireland we had known begin to disintegrate. The fall of O'Neill, the rampant fundamentalism of Paisley and the Unionist 'Old Guard' blocked all political progress, which in turn led to the rise of the Provisional IRA and the Loyalist paramilitaries. While the security forces tried to hold the ring, the political process faltered and then failed, with resultant widespread suffering and heartbreak among the people of both main communities.

One of the hardest jobs as a front-line reporter was to witness the suffering of the innocents, to record the pain and despair, and yet it was moving to witness the nobility of many of those who had suffered most. I was privileged and honoured to know the late Senator Gordon Wilson and his family, and to write his life-story with its courage and hope. He was taken from us far too soon, but his words of forgiveness still shine as a beacon in the darkness.

As well as reporting on events, I gave my personal support to a number of organisations which worked imaginatively for peace, in their different ways. They included the Corrymeela Community, Co-operation North (now Co-operation Ireland), and the Dutch-Irish Peace Advisory Group, which is no longer with us.

At a local level, I joined my fellow members in a Presbyterian Church in troubled North Belfast in holding out the hand of friendship to local Roman Catholic congregations. This has led to regular meetings, including joint Bible Study - in other words peace sharing at the grass-roots. Recently a nearby Catholic chapel was burned down by arsonists. On the next Sunday our church had a collection for our Catholic neighbours, without our knowing that, on the very night before, somebody had tried unsuccessfully to set fire to our own church. Such is the reality of sectarianism in the area where I live.

I have set down the above observations with almost a sense of wonder that we have survived so much in Northern Ireland, and yet the will for peace lives on. There are many times when one is cast into despair - not least in the unspeakable act of someone trying to burn people out of their homes, and to burn down their church - literally an incursion upon holy ground. And yet we get strength to carry on.

Thus, peace-making for me has been more than a cerebral exercise, or an academic blue-print. It has been central to my life as a journalist and as a peace-making citizen of Northern Ireland, living in an unfashionable area which seems to generate only bad news - despite the good news between the lines. What have I learned from the past thirty years ?

As a journalist I have come to realise even more that good news is harder to project than bad. My first book, about the Corrymeela Community, did well but it did not sell as many copies as a local journalist's grisly account of the Shankill Butchers, a gang of Loyalist hoodlums who picked up innocent Catholics at random and murdered them. There is a fascination with evil, and, sadly, good news stories about peace-making are less riveting. As a consequence, peace-makers have to battle against the cynicism of others, and their facile accusations that they are merely 'do-gooders'.

Secondly, I have learned that many people talk a good peace plan but few can carry it out. Over the past thirty years Northern Ireland has been the most analysed piece of earth in Europe, if not the world. Whole generations of journalists, academics and politicians have made their careers out of it, but a facility with words alone is not the key to peace-making.

Some of the best peace-makers say very little. They listen, and that is a key to making peace. A good listener, and there are few enough of them, develops trust because in listening there is no self-seeking or self-aggrandisement. When the ego gives way to reflection and a search for the common good, strange things begin to happen.

Thirdly, I have learned that peace cannot be built from the top-down. On occasions it is important to have a grand, if complex, master-plan such as the Good Friday Agreement. But it cannot work fully unless there is support from the bottom-up.

One of the hopes for peace in Northern Ireland is the way in which politicians from all parties have learned to work together, of necessity, in local councils. They are discovering slowly that if they want to make progress in schemes, large or small, they have to work together. By doing so they begin to build trust, even grudgingly, and strange things again start to happen.

Significantly, I have learned also that peace-making begins in your own head. I particularly remember two comments, from the many I have reported over all the years. One was from an Ulsterman who said *"Unless you can make peace in your own home, you have no right to try to make peace in Ireland."* The other came from a Dutch peace-maker who said *"Once you start to 'give in', you also start to win."* It took me years to figure that out, personally and professionally.

Finally, I have learned that peace begins with one hand-shake, one smile, or one kind act across the divide. On the morning after our church had been damaged by vandals several years ago - long before the latest attack - the first person on the scene was the local Catholic priest Canon Hugh Murphy, bearing a cheque and - more important - his condolences and those of his parishioners. That act of thoughtfulness and solidarity said more about peace-making than a thousand sermons or academic theses or political statements.

That first step across the divide requires courage, but is the only way. The world may never understand why the peace-makers shall be called *"blessed"*, nor do the peace-makers need to know this themselves. All they need to do is to get on with it, at all times and at all levels, but particularly where the pain is sharpest and where the going is toughest. As A. J. Muste once noted *"There is no way to peace - peace is the way"*.

I do not feel obliged to believe that the same God who has endowed us with sense, reason and intellect has intended us to forgo their use.

Galileo Galilei

True Peace
Enda McDonagh

Enda McDonagh is a priest of the archdiocese of Tuam.

A s the names of the victims of conflict are recalled, the sense of darkness seems overwhelming, the sense that we were a people still walking in the dark on a bleak mid-winter's night. Out of these depths we can only cry to you, O Lord. And yet we must listen also. Lest our cry become self-centred, self-pitying, we must listen and watch and wait.

The light that the poet-prophet Isaiah promised God's first people, Israel, seven hundred years ago, came into this world two thousand years ago as the Gospel of John reminds us, *"the darkness did not comprehend the light"*. The angels and the shepherds did comprehend as they rejoiced in the birth of him whom Isaiah had designated Prince of Peace. They proclaimed the message the whole world wanted to hear: 'Peace on earth'. As Isaiah had promised, *"all the footgear of battle/ Every cloak rolled in blood/ is burnt/ and consumed by fire/ For there is a child born for us.."* who *"will wield authority over the nations"* and *"these will hammer their swords into ploughshares/ their spears into sickles"*. A vision for the world, a mission of the Prince of Peace and a mission far from complete even on this tiny territory of Northern Ireland, ground hallowed by such disciples as Columba and Patrick and so many others, ground now desecrated, stained, as all the earth is stained, by the precious blood of so many daughters and sons of God.

As we wait and watch we wonder like T.S. Eliot's three kings: have we come all this way for birth or death? For peace or war or at best vulnerable cease-fire? The same problem must have worried the sky-god in Seamus Heaney's poem. It certainly cannot have escaped the attention of the creator-covenant God of Abraham and Moses or the creator-redeemer God of Isaiah and his promised suffering Messiah, the Messiah we know as Jesus Christ. In the beginning, in the creating of the heavens and the earth, the creator God knew the risks involved. Sharing divine freedom with the fickle human race might well end in tears, murderous, fratricidal tears. So it did with Cain and Abel and the countless generations to follow. Our Irish tradition of brother slaying brother is sadly not exceptional in human history. Indeed at first reading of that history it might seem the rule, the inevitable law of reprisal and retaliation. An eye for an eye, justice, just war, justified killing in self defence before mercy or forgiveness. Before love of enemies, before the Christ-child was, before the Christ-adult died, praying 'Father forgive them', the whole biblical story is the story of the risks God took for his destructive people and his fragile cosmos. Of the risks he took for *shalom*, the flourishing together of the whole human race and all creation, *shalom* the Hebrew word translated, peace. By this shall the world know the story of our God, that we love one another in the basic and transforming sense that we live in peace with one another. A risky and costly mission. Nobody knew that better than God's own son.

The thirty years of Jesus' earthly life has many echoes for family and friends of the thirty years Northern Ireland has recently endured. These have been the years of suffering, of testing almost to the point of despair, 'My God,

My God…', but not quite. Hope grounded finally in Easter Sunday was first manifest in a stable in Bethlehem. A hope that could not be extinguished, God would not forsake his people and enough people knew that to keep hope for peace alive, to let justice and peace embrace, to let hope and history rhyme.

We have had dinned into us, and we need the lesson, that peace is a process that is always in the making and so we remain fearful of the unmaking. For that unmaking we would all be culpable. So what shall Jesus' disciples do to foster the making and prevent the unmaking? What risks are we prepared to take for peace in response to the God who risked all for our peace? Shall we stay in our comfortable clerical establishments with our coffee-cup ecumenism and our soothing clichés or shall we break out of our sacred cloisters as God broke out of the divine enclosure? Shall we enter into the smelly, nasty stable to cleanse it of religious superiority, prejudice and exclusion? And perhaps pay the price of God in Jesus paid. And if we do not, who shall carry the angels' message of peace?

Before we become depressed by the task ahead, let us recall that peace is a gift before it is a task, or even a process, and a divine gift at that. The process is also a divine gift entrusted to human hands - dirty, imperfect human hands. Clay-shaping hands, crop-growing hands, hands that are meant for ploughshares rather than swords or guns, for ploughing and cultivating earth rather than gunning down a neighbour, for greeting and blessing rather than rejecting and cursing. All human life with all its ambiguities is in our hands, to embrace or to kill, to create or to destroy.

Peace as a gift, task and process requires creative hands and minds and hearts. That work of human hands we call the gun could be turned into an earth-nurturing ploughshare or a life giving surgical instrument or a beautiful sculpture if we had the will and the skill to do so. Our unskilled hands and our unwilling hearts may have to unlearn some of their old bad habits before we become true creators of peace. This is the time to unlearn the old and to relearn the new as the angels' melody lingers. This is the time to recognise in symbol our stage on the way and the miles to go before we sleep in heavenly peace. This is the time to symbolise the distance come and still to go, to symbolise our hope in the refashioning of the guns, not yet to ploughshares, but out of gun-hood and into a kind of nest for doves of peace, the Spirit of peace, always with us in Emmanuel terms, if we are willing to take the risks. This is the night the outcry of suffering and dying becomes the birth-cry of new life, of new hope, of true peace.

Peace

Catherine McGeachy

*Catherine McGeachy is Managing Director of Vision Consultants Ltd.
Catherine's work is dedicated to promoting human potential, individually
and collectively, in the workplace.*

To sit, surrounded by emergent Spring
Infused by Life and the Song it sings
To hear the silence and the sound of a bee ...
This is peace

To drink, unintruded, of Nature's beauty
And experience her calm and bring this in the City
And breathe in Her air, laden with fragrance ...
This is peace

To contemplate Life, with a view of the sea
To watch a flight of birds in balletic choreography
To hear the swish of the trees and the rush of the shore ...
This is peace

To watch two swallows chase one another
And to gaze on two butterflies dancing together
To watch the birds teach their young to fly ...
This is peace

To have faced anxiety, fear and doubt
With a heart full of courage, God' Word and stout
In belief that Love is indeed all powerful ...
This is peace

God, help us not to despise or oppose what we do not understand

William Penn

Supporting Peace But Not The Process
Anthony McIntyre

Anthony McIntyre is a republican writer who served over eighteen years in prison for involvement in the armed struggle of the Provisional Irish Republican Army. He lives in Belfast and at present works on a project known as 'The Blanket' which challenges censorship and explores political ideas.

Quite recently I attended a debate at which Jim Gibney of Sinn Féin was a panellist. I listened while he told his audience that ten years ago it was not possible to mention the word 'peace' within the Republican movement. Brian Feeney, another panellist, quickly corrected him pointing out that peace documents had been produced by Sinn Féin in 1987. Had Feeney so chosen, he could have gone back considerably further. 'Peace' was a term much used by the Provisional IRA's first chief of staff, the late Sean MacStiofain, and he vacated that position as early as 1972 underlining the elongated shelf life a peace discourse actually does have within Provisional republicanism.

Those who inhabit a culture where authoritarian power is virtually the centre of gravity, and as Eric Hoffer pointed out, those in possession of such power cannot only lie but can make their lies come true. It is regrettable but hardly surprising that these people, while fundamentally decent and honest, would serve as a conduit through which an authoritarian leadership would demand that the world accept how it alone had worked strenuously for peace. All preceding it was incompetent; all outside of it reactionary and devoid of any strategic vision. Anyone asking a difficult question ought, therefore, to be ashamed - such probing was unhelpful to the peace process.

Up until the arrest of three republican activists in Colombia, a large self-emasculated element within the media world facilitated Sinn Féin on these matters preferring to ask the easy question designed to ensure a soft landing for those republicans 'helpful' to the peace process. The same element further endeavoured to deliberately position the term 'dissident republican' in a bedrock of violence. Taking the principle of *'definitio est negatio'* (to define is to limit) to the extreme, there emerged an illusory binary construct in which Sinn Féin stood for peace and dissidents for war.

As a republican dissident I found the time and effort refuting such insinuations tiresome. The attempt by Sinn Féin to monopolise peace and exclusively articulate it to the party's own brand of republicanism was patently false. The contextualisation of dissident republicans as both monolithic and hermetically sealed off from anything but violence was always self-serving. It allowed a wider world to turn a blind eye to Provisional IRA use of force on the basis that the alternative was always likely to be something worse.

And yet republican dissidents such as Tommy Gorman and myself have stood firm against any suggestion that republicanism should engage in violence. At one point we argued that never again should it take life in pursuit of its goals. Two nights later our homes were picketed by Sinn Féin who took exception to that line of thinking. It seemed to us that while we supported the peace, Sinn Féin only supported the process. Hardly a recipe for a lasting stability in any society.

So what can peace mean for a dissident republican? Firstly, while desirable, it is not essential to get rid of the British to have peace. But while they remain and oversee projects such as the Good Friday Agreement the foundations upon which peace can be built shall always remain suspect. Such a project entrenches rather than overcomes sectarianism. It may unite the chattering classes as they pursue the interests of their own bloc. But because any progress - always measured against the opposing bloc - is dependent on communal advances, the chattering classes only manage to drive those on the ground further apart in a self-perpetuating sectarian spiral.

More broadly, Ireland is a society facing economic recession and increased racial tension. Peace must confront those issues. If it is not based on democracy that redistributes wealth and is inclusive of all nationalities and races, then is it a peace worth having? Peace is not the absence of war. All too often those promulgating peace ignore what Dom Helder Camara of Brazil once termed 'structural violence' such as poverty which denies human dignity and development.

What is paramount is the need for a human rights regime underpinned by a democratic international law which is not a tool of the rich and powerful. This captures the essence of both Fergal Keane and Jacques Derrida when they argue respectively that *"the human rights culture of our age makes the impossible seem possible"* and that *"democracy ... is the political experience of the impossible".* The twinning of these concepts compels us to avoid both apathy and tuning into the monotonous chant of the *status quo* – 'there is no alternative'.

Such a vision can only develop if we have the means to visualise through structures of transparency and dissent. Peace and democracy cannot otherwise survive. Without these structures the likelihood increases that Ireland may produce a situation similar to that pertaining in Austria where there was never a great tradition of dissenting structures. Consequently, the right wing populist Jorg Haider came to power with all the ominous potential for racial havoc and devastation therein. Are we to be so afraid of democratic experimentation that we succumb to the 'castrated democracy' of Chile about which the dissident writer Ariel Dorfman had this to say:

> *"What politicians have done in Chile is that they've made democracy fragile by saying it's so fragile we can't touch it. Well, no. You've got to bring people into the process of defining democracy, testing it and pushing it. If you don't it's not true democracy."*

Republican dissidents who reject the prevailing orthodoxy and dissent from the use of physical force can do much for peace and democracy. More, perhaps, than those who talk peace but do not actually live it.

Peace in the North
Tommy McKearney

Tommy McKearney is a former member of the Irish Republican Army (IRA) who served sixteen years in prison in Northern Ireland. He now works for Expac in Monaghan, helping former prisoners resettle post release. He is also Editor of the radical republican magazine, 'Fourthwrite' and writes for the cross-community quarterly, 'The Other View'.

P eace - like a cure for cancer or an end to famine - has universal and unqualified approval. No known politician, clergyman, trade unionist, journalist or even soldier is on record as being opposed to peace *per se*. This is not to say that, given certain circumstances, any or all of the above might endorse or even participate in the bloodiest of conflicts.

The difficulty about peace is that it manifests itself as a consequence of events, treaties and agreements rather than existing as an organic commodity or a product that can be artificially manufactured. Consequently, it is possible to talk in seemingly oxymoronic terms of: *armed campaigns of pacification*, wars to *achieve or restore peace* and to describe armies of dangerously armed men as *peace keeping forces*. The potential for paradox in all of this was well recognised by the ancient Roman Tacitus when he wrote of, *making a wilderness and calling it peace*.

It is essential therefore when examining Northern Ireland (or any other area of conflict) that we avoid the seductive temptation to view the conflict as a struggle between peace loving (and hence right thinking people) on one hand and war mongering, men of violence on the other. The weakness

163

within such an oversimplification is compounded when commentators attempt to create an additional *non sequitor* by insisting that in order to fit into the peace loving camp, it is necessary to uncritically endorse a particular viewpoint or even a specific treaty or agreement.

A recent example of this in Ireland is the bi-governmentally endorsed consensus created around the Good Friday Agreement (GFA). So passionate are some of its supporters that they become frighteningly aggressive when critics highlight the inconsistencies of the document, shades perhaps of the old story about an opinion poll taken in Turkey that discovered a 95% majority in favour of democracy, while simultaneously 85% of those polled believed that the dissenting 5% should be shot for holding anti-democratic opinions.

At the risk of falling foul of a somewhat similar outlook, it remains necessary to point out the limitations of the political process in Northern Ireland.

Peace, as stated above, is dependent on many things but above all it is essential that all parties to any settlement agree on the key and fundamental details of what is proposed. In South Africa, for example, there was a clear understanding that in return for retaining the economic *status quo* and observing a policy of no retaliation, the white minority would surrender political power to the majority. There were many on both sides who felt this arrangement was wrong but all understood what was on offer.

In the North no such clarity is evident. The key constitutional issue has not been resolved in spite of claims to the contrary. David Trimble and his allies have recommended the GFA to unionists on the basis that it guarantees the continued existence of the 'Union'. At the same time Sinn Féin has assured its supporters that the GFA will lead in short order to a United Ireland. So confident indeed is the party president, Gerry Adams, that he has even mentioned the year 2016.

Common sense tells us both cannot be correct and that one side or the other must eventually be disappointed. How disappointed remains to be seen, but the view that given enough time the loser will forget what he was fighting about is surely a risky proposition.

Several other areas of disagreement within the GFA highlight just how risky this may be. Although apparently recently addressed, the important issues of decommissioning and policing remain contentious. Republicans feel that they were bulldozed into retreating beyond what they signed up to on the original eponymous Good Friday. Nor is scepticism confined to one side, as is evidenced by the contortions the Stormont Assembly has undergone in order to re-elect the First and Deputy First Minister. And that is before we look at the wider elements of rejectionist unionism mounting pickets on primary schools or throwing pipe bombs.

Nevertheless, there is undoubtedly a great desire for peace in Northern Ireland. After almost thirty years of bloodshed, this is hardly surprising. The very duration however, gives us a clue to the apparent paradox of a greatly reduced level of physical conflict with no corresponding universal endorsement from within the unionist community. The fact is that the crucial area of dispute - the value or existence of Northern Ireland - remains unresolved.

A majority of unionists remain convinced that Northern Ireland is a separate entity from the rest of Ireland, entitled to go whatever way its majority chooses, even if this entails excluding republicans and nationalists. Simultaneously, republicans and nationalists still refuse to accept the permanence of the six county zone and are, at best, prepared to wait a little while longer before terminating the northern political entity. The positions are mutually irreconcilable and there is unfortunately a degree of accuracy in the observation that peace in Northern Ireland is founded as much by exhaustion as by a deep running conviction in the merits of Senator Mitchell's document.

What makes the Northern Ireland situation well nigh impossible to resolve is the absence of one of the vital requirements to ending any long running dispute - a rough equivalence of forces guaranteeing mutual disadvantage to both if conflict continues or resumes. Britain, in spite of its claim to have no selfish or strategic interest in Ireland, continues to guarantee the permanence of the 'Union' while a majority supports it. The position of Northern Ireland within the U.K. (the core value of unionism after all) is therefore safeguarded whether unionists share power or not. For unionists this is a 'win, win' situation thus discouraging any meaningful compromise.

A possible parallel with the relationship between Britain and Northern Irish unionism is that between Washington and Tel Aviv.

Ultimately, a proper and lasting peace will only come about in Northern Ireland when steps are taken to overcome the key element of irreconcilibility. To allow this to take place it is necessary to remove the impediment to progress created by the connection with Britain? And for those who point to the inevitability of civil war and genocide in the event of Britain severing its links, let us point to a proposal made over a quarter of a century ago by leading loyalists and unionists. Prominent Ulster Volunteer Force (UVF) members and a powerful member of the Northern Ireland legal profession mooted the idea of a confederation on this island. A solution that would break the connection with Britain, allow for a rough balance of forces and communities in the six-counties and create structures to prevent Dublin dictating events in the North.

Perhaps that would be the sort of agreement that would give us all - Wolfe Tone included - real peace.

This country will not be a good place for any of us to live in unless
we make it a good place for all of us to live in.

Theodore Roosevelt

Lessons for the Future
George Mitchell

Senator George J. Mitchell was appointed to the United States Senate in 1980. Mitchell was elected to his first full term in 1982 and was re-elected in 1988. Senator Mitchell served in the Senate for 14 years, including six as the Senate Majority Leader. Senator Mitchell serves as the Chancellor of the Queens University of Northern Ireland and as the President of the Economic Club of Washington. Senator Mitchell served as Chairman of the Peace Negotiations in Northern Ireland. Under his leadership an historic accord, ending decades of conflict, was agreed to by the Governments of Ireland and the United Kingdom and the political parties of Northern Ireland. In May 1998 the Agreement was overwhelmingly endorsed by the voters of Ireland, North and South, in a referendum.

My involvement in the peace process in Northern Ireland was at once very demanding and deeply rewarding. Since my return to the United States, following the reaching of an accord - widely known as the Good Friday Agreement - I've been asked often what lessons Northern Ireland holds for other conflicts. What follows is my answer to that question.

I begin with caution. Each human being is unique, as is each society. It follows logically, then, that no two conflicts are the same. Much as we would like it, there is no magic formula which, once discovered, can be used to end all conflicts.

But there are certain principles which arise out of my experience in Northern Ireland that I believe are universal.

First, I believe there's no such thing as a conflict that can't be ended. They're created and sustained by human beings. They can be ended by human beings. No matter how ancient the conflict, no matter how hurtful, peace can prevail.

When I arrived in Northern Ireland I found, to my dismay, a widespread feeling of pessimism among the public and the political leaders. It's a small, well-informed society where I quickly became well known. Every day people would stop me on the street, in the airport, in a restaurant. They always began with kind words: *"Thank you Senator." "God bless you." "We appreciate what you're trying to do."* But they always ended in despair. *"You're wasting your time." "This conflict can't be ended." "We've been killing each other for centuries and we're doomed to go on killing each other forever."*

As best I could, I worked to reverse such attitudes. This is the special responsibility of political leaders, from whom many in the public take their cue. Leaders must lead. And one way is to create an attitude of success, the belief that problems can be solved, that things can be better. Not in a foolish or unrealistic way, but in a way that creates hope and confidence among the people.

A second need is for a clear and determined policy not to yield to the men of violence. Over and over they tried to destroy the peace process in Northern Ireland; at times they nearly succeeded.

In July 1998, three young Catholic boys were burned to death as they slept. A month later a devastating bomb in Omagh killed twenty-nine people and injured 300, Protestant and Catholic alike. These were acts of appalling ignorance and hatred. They must be totally condemned. But to succumb to the temptation to retaliate would give criminals what they want: escalating sectarian violence and the end of the peace process. The way to respond is to swiftly bring those who committed these crimes to justice and go forward in peace. That means there must be an endless supply of patience and perseverance. Sometimes the mountains seem so high and rivers so wide that it is hard to continue the journey. But no matter how bleak the outlook, the search for peace must go on.

Seeking an end to conflict is not for the timid or the tentative. It takes courage, perseverance and steady nerves in the face of violence. I believe it a mistake to say in advance that if acts of violence occur the negotiations will stop. That's an invitation to those who use violence to destroy the peace process, and it transfers control of the agenda from the peaceful majority to the violent minority.

A third need is a willingness to compromise. Peace and political stability cannot be achieved in sharply divided societies unless there is a genuine willingness to understand the other point of view and enter into principled compromise. That is easy to say, but very hard to do, because it requires of political leaders that they take risks for peace.

Most political leaders dislike risk-taking of any kind. Most get to be leaders by minimizing risk. To ask them, in the most difficult and dangerous of circumstances, to be bold is asking much.

But it must be asked of them, and they must respond, if there is to be hope for peace. I know it can be done, because I saw it first-hand in Northern Ireland. Men and women, some of whom had never before met, never before spoken, who had spent their entire lives in conflict, came together in an agreement for peace. Admittedly, it was long and difficult. But it did happen. And if it happened there, it can happen elsewhere.

A fourth principle is to recognize that the implementation of agreements is as difficult, and as important, as reaching them. That should be self-evident. But often just getting an agreement is so difficult that the natural tendency is to celebrate, then go home and relax. But as we are now seeing in Northern Ireland, in the Middle East, in the Balkans, getting it done is often harder than agreeing to do it.

Once again, patience and perseverance are necessary. It is especially important that our citizens, busy at home and all across the world, not be distracted, or become complacent by the good feeling created by a highly publicized agreement. If a conflict is important enough to get involved in, it must be seen through all the way to a fair and successful conclusion.

It will take extraordinary determination and commitment to get safely through all of the remaining problems. But I believe it can be done and will be done. It would be an immense tragedy were the process to fail now. The British and Irish Governments and the political leaders of Northern Ireland have come too far to let peace slip away.

The people of Northern Ireland deserve better than the troubles they've had over the past several decades. Peace and political stability are not too much to ask for. They are minimal needs for a decent and caring society.

There's a final point that to me is so important that it extends beyond open conflict. I recall clearly my first day in Northern Ireland six years ago. I saw for the first time the huge wall which physically separates the communities in Belfast. Thirty feet high, topped in places with barbed wire, it is an ugly reminder of the intensity and duration of the conflict. Ironically, it's called 'The Peace Line'.

On that first morning I met with Catholics on their side of the wall, in the afternoon with Protestants on their side. Their messages had not been coordinated, but they were the same: in Belfast, they told me, there is a high correlation between unemployment and violence. They said that where men and women have no opportunity, no hope, they are more likely to take the path of violence.

As I sat and listened to them, I thought that I could just as easily be in Chicago or Calcutta or Johannesburg or in the Middle East. Despair is the fuel of instability and conflict everywhere. Hope is essential to peace and stability. Men and women everywhere need income to support their families, and they need the satisfaction of doing something worthwhile and meaningful with their lives.

The conflict in Northern Ireland is obviously not exclusively or even primarily economic. It involves religion and national identity: the majority identify with and want to become part of the United Kingdom; the minority identify with and want to become part of a united Ireland. The Good Friday Agreement acknowledges the legitimacy of both aspirations. And it creates the possibility that economic prosperity will flow from and contribute to lasting peace.

My most fervent hope is that history will record that, despite some continuing violence and discord, the Troubles really ended at Omagh, that the bomb which shattered the calm of that warm summer afternoon was the last spasm of a long and violent conflict. Amidst the death and destruction, there was laid bare the utter senselessness of trying to solve the political problems of Northern Ireland by violence. It won't work. It will only make things worse.

Two weeks later I accompanied Prime Minister Blair and President Clinton to Omagh to meet with the survivors and the relatives of the dead. There were hundreds of people present. Among them two with whom I spoke and who I will never forget. Claire Gallagher was fifteen years old, tall and lovely, an aspiring pianist. She lost both of her eyes. As we spoke, she sat, with two large white patches where her eyes used to be, an exemplar of grace and courage. Michael Monaghan was thirty-three years old. He lost his wife, who was pregnant, their eighteen-month daughter and his wife's mother; three generations wiped out in a single, senseless moment. Michael was left with three children under the age of five. One of them, Patrick, two years old, asks his father every day: *"When's Mommy coming home?"*

Despite their terrible and irreparable loss, both Claire and Michael urged that the peace process go forward. Their courage gave me hope. Their determination gave me resolve.

I am not objective. I'm deeply biased in favour of the people of Northern Ireland. Having spent six years among them, I've come to like and admire them. While they can be quarrelsome and too quick to take offense, they are also warm and generous, energetic and productive.

They've made mistakes but they're learning from them. They're learning that violence won't solve their problems; that unionists and nationalists have more in common than they have differences; that knowledge of their history is a good thing, but being chained to the past is not.

There will be many setbacks along the way, but the direction for Northern Ireland was firmly set when the people approved the Good Friday Agreement in referendum. The people there are sick of war. They're sick of so many funerals, especially those involving the small white coffins of children, prematurely laid into the rolling green fields of their beautiful countryside. They want peace, and I hope they can keep it.

When the agreement was reached, at about six o'clock on the evening of April 10, we had been in negotiations for nearly two years and continuously for about the last forty hours. We were elated and exhausted. In my parting comments I told them that the agreement was, for me, the realization of a dream that had sustained me for three and a half years, the longest, most difficult years of my life. Now, I said, I have a new dream. It is to return to Northern Ireland in a few years with my young son. We will roam the country, taking in the sights and sounds of that lovely land. Then, on a rainy afternoon, we will drive to Stormont and sit quietly in the visitors gallery in the Northern Ireland Assembly.

There we will watch and listen as the members debate the ordinary issues of life in a democratic society - education, health care, tourism, a culture. There will be no talk of war, for the war will be long over. There will be no talk of peace, for peace will be taken for granted. On that day, the day on which peace is taken for granted in Northern Ireland, I will be fulfilled and people of goodwill everywhere will rejoice.

Peace, Politics and Principles

Noel Mulcahy

*Noel Mulcahy is Emeritus Professor of Industrial Strategy at the
University of Limerick and served as a Senator from 1977 until 1981.*

W hen the Irish Peace Institute was established I was invited me to become involved, and I refused because, as I said at the time, *"I have enough conflict to deal with in the emergent University to do me for a while"*. But that decision did not deter me from reflecting on the issues. I use the word 'reflecting' in a very special way; the way that the philosopher Bernard Lonergan taught me mainly through his study of *Insight* (1957). Essentially, Lonergan distinguishes between common sense knowing and scientific knowing; the former has to do with understanding on the basis of one's experience, the latter has to do with theory, and in particular understanding through the study of the *relationship* between concepts used to describe or measure aspects of society or systems.

As a Senator I had had experience of politics at a number of levels, including chairing the Irish Oireachtas interparty committee on Arab Affairs, which had a special interest in the Palestine/Israel question. As a lecturer in the Irish Management Institute (IMI), University College Dublin and Trinity College, I dealt with theories of conflict analysis from a theoretical point of view.

While preparing a paper to be delivered at a Congressional Club lunch in Washington (1995) and consulting Bernard Crick's book *In Defence of Politics*

(1964) I was struck by the absence of media argument about political science theories which might be adduced to help to guide politicians in dealing with the Northern Ireland question. It seemed to me that Crick's seminal thoughts provided a theoretical foundation to help to understand the problem process. Coming from this point of view I wrote a number of papers and articles that I shared with individuals who were active in what had become to be known as the Peace Process. These included three Taoisigh, Ministers, Hume, Adams, McLaughlin, Congress Members (King, Gilman, Neill, Costello), numerous civil servants and media people. The Limerick Leader published the original piece and one follow-up after my White House visit. The Independent used a letter which was a rebuttal of an attack by Arnold and Cruise O'Brien on Albert Reynolds, who had taken up the line I was advocating, for the rest- silence. Nobody wanted to consider the proposition - when governance is the issue politics precedes democracy. In other words - the guiding principles of politics are super ordinate to the guiding principles of democracy when attempting to put an agreed structure of governance in place.

In March 1970 at a seminar in the IMI, Professor Dale A. Henning introduced us to a framework for the 'analysis of difference'. I have been using it since then. It works.

Imagine a matrix frame made up of *columns* with headings - goals, facts, methods, values and *rows* headed by - education, perception, role. This analytical framework may be used in a structured way to examine the nature of the difference between conflicting groups. In this short essay I cannot illustrate fully how this works for Unionist - v - Nationalist positions. But the issues arising from such an analysis should be obvious. Clearly it lends itself to discussion on the elements of the difference, one at a time, without jumping from one point to another with the 'a but what about? ' Where difference exists and cannot be changed (as of now) then accept the position. In other cases the differences may be mediated. In any event the nature of the difference, being better understood, might lend itself to change over time. Of course, in the case of the heading 'goals', the clashing objectives in some way have to be lived with; unionist aims and nationalist aims are directly opposed. The heading 'method' lends itself to some innovation; is there a method or system of working or administration which might accommodate what can't be changed and might help to bring about a convergence of the things that can? There are many echoes of these sentiments to be detected in the Mitchell Report, especially under the heading 'values'.

The search for an acceptable method switches us back to Bernard Crick. Having read and reread *In Defence of Politics*, I made the following assertion in my Limerick Leader article (1996) and again in the Independent (1997)

> *"in any territory where the governance is being questioned by a significant proportion of the population, agreement on a compromise system of governance must be mediated by a political process involving all concerned. This political process must be allowed to happen regardless of the prior behaviour of the differing parties. Once a modified system of governing is agreed then democracy can commence. In this context* **politics precedes democracy***".*

The agreed government can proceed to deal with the other factors in the equation. Bernard Crick attended a seminar at the University of Limerick in 1996, and he agreed with this interpretation of his broader theses.

Having reflected on these various insights, it was, and still is, clear that the cause of the many differences between groups in Northern Ireland, including violence (which was not justified anyway), was the lack of agreed governance - John Hume's 'agreed solution'. If by some magical or miraculous process a formula for governance could be constructed which would allow the main goals of the contesting groups to be accommodated, that would be the unique solution which then would be superordinate to all other wants - including dealing with arms of any kind, and policing.

The almost incredible happened despite the sceptics. The Good Friday Agreement is inherently a commitment to a form of governance (and the word governance should be more often used to describe it) involving a democratically elected assembly, a cabinet of ministers and other mechanisms. In the case of Northern Ireland, the simplicity and elegance of the argument is complicated by the (necessary) retention of some powers by the super-superordinate government in London and to some extent in Dublin. It is understandable, but unfortunate, that certain factors were made equal or conditional for the acceptance of the governance, e.g. decommissioning and policing.

It was with great pain and dismay that I sat at the Irish American Tony O' Reilly dinner in Washington on St Patrick's Day 1995 and heard our

Taoiseach Bruton expressing great satisfaction with the Framework Document and the ceasefires, but committing to the notion of 'prior decommissioning'. He should have said something like - we must now seek to put in place a new governance and we must make it work (and it has!) and let nothing undermine it. It was Weick who said that we enact the world through the words we use; if we sing the song of decommissioning and not the song of governance we will have no governance and no peace. Of course the putting of arms beyond use is important and should be pursued, but not at the expense of the ceasefires and governance. By this analysis the lack of agreed governance was the prime and root cause of all the Northern Ireland problems, including violence. The London political and administrative leaders should be made to understand that thesis, so that Reid and Blair will not be tempted to back down. Blair must not be another Wilson.

I hear the reader saying - but what about now, 9 October 2001? I say that the analysis holds good. Maintain the governance against all the objections. It is the superordinate goal. Its absence will cause another cycle of conflict. Get agreement that putting arms beyond use will take place over a period of ten years under the administration of General De Chastelain, and get Sinn Féin to agree to work the police authority, with a promise to review the system every three years. The ten years could be negotiable, but not less than five years. And let peace prevail.

I have attempted in this essay to show how three different theoretical constructs can be used to understand the determinants of this great puzzle, and, having understood, to provide some guidance on how to proceed. My diagnosis may be flawed. In any event I thank Lonergan, Crick and Henning for the inspiration.

A Travellers Tale

Dominic Murray

> *Professor Dominic Murray was born in Northern Ireland. He was educated in St McNissis College Garrontower and attended the University of Ulster where he graduated with a Higher Diploma in Education and a First Class Honours Bachelors Degree in Science. He was awarded a Doctorate in 1983. He has taught at secondary, teacher training and university levels in Northern Ireland and the Republic of Ireland. Professor Murray is currently Professor of Peace and Co-operation Studies and Director of the Centre for Peace and Development Studies at the University of Limerick.*

In 1980 I left Northern Ireland to take up a position in University College Cork. At that time, I left a State which was characterised by an abundance of security measures, a minimum of trust and a total lack of communication. Nearly half of the population were fearful of change while the other half felt they were excluded from the process of major decision-making and did not identify with what, in other circumstances, might be seen as the normal facets of governance. Policing is an example.

I arrived in a State where social behaviour seemed still to be affected by a civil war which had taken place sixty years previously. In terms of major decision-making, it seemed to me that the Roman Catholic Church had an unhealthy influence on the process at almost every level. Irish identity appeared to be introspective in nature and measured principally in terms of the degree to which one was anti-British.

In the 1980's there was little social or recreational contact at a cross border level. Comparatively few travelled south and even less made the perceived perilous journey north. It is hardly surprising therefore that mutual perceptions tended to be stereotypical and less than cordial in nature. There existed a strong Unionist conviction that the Republic of Ireland could be seen in terms of a 'sleeping lion' waiting to pounce if defences were lowered, even marginally. Hence the 'not an inch' strategy. In the Republic of Ireland on the other hand, there seemed to be a general fear that the 'malaise' in the north might spread southwards. Far from acquisitiveness, the general public knew remarkably little about Northern Ireland and cared even less about it. If pushed, people generally would express total amazement at how anyone could identify with the old enemy (perfidious Albion). For them therefore, the solution to Northern Ireland's problems was simply to convince Unionists of the errors of their ways and of the self-evident benefits of a united Ireland. What interested me at that time, and now, was that these stereotypes were as strongly held as they were ill-informed, ill-conceived and incorrect.

The request to write this little piece has forced me to think of the developments since 1980 and made me acutely aware of the remarkable changes that have taken place in each jurisdiction since then. In the Republic of Ireland for example, the hegemony of the Roman Catholic Church, as I perceived it, has decreased significantly. This has been partly due to a commitment on the part of that church and partly forced upon it by other well-publicised events. I feel that this has had the general affect of permitting, not only a broadening of people's minds, but also allowing for increased awareness of cultural mores and morals at a global level. At about the same time, we had the phenomenon of Riverdance which, among other things, increased global awareness of Ireland. I believe that the synthesis of this increased awareness, both of and by the Irish people, has promoted the development of the concept of identity there. Gone is the old anti-British criterion to be replaced by a pride and confidence in being Irish. This newfound confidence has played no little part in the nurturing of the Celtic Tiger.

In Northern Ireland the changes have been no less remarkable. While violence is continuing, it is at a level of an order of magnitude less than when I left in 1980. Security checks at shop entrances and on the public highways are almost a thing of the past. There remain of course important and major difficulties, not least of which are decommissioning, policing etc.. But the important thing is we now have a forum for communication. People who had never done so before are now talking to each other, both at a civic level and also in the Northern Ireland Assembly, which was established as part of the Good Friday Agreement. It seems to me that the main task of the Assembly, if it survives, will be to attempt to moderate the different definitions of identity which exist in Northern Ireland and also accommodate to the differing perceptions of nationhood. Also, as a result of the Agreement, cross border contact and communication has increased dramatically, both at formal and informal levels. I hope that, at the very least, this will enlighten the previously ill-informed stereotypes.

However, I believe that it is the advancing economies in both Northern Ireland and the Republic of Ireland which are likely to play the most important role in the future development of the Ireland of the future. As the concept of the global village becomes evermore a reality, Europe will obviously become our nearest suburb. It will be important for both jurisdictions, not only to react to, but also to anticipate the economic and other demands that will be made on them from outside. It is likely that the best way they can do this will be at a co-operative level. For this reason I believe that if unity is to come about on the island, it will be at a pragmatic rather than political level. It will be an entity far removed from the romantic dream of previous centuries, but will rather emerge as a reality to which the majority can not only subscribe to, but also identify with.

What is Truth?

David Norris

David Norris is an independent Senator representing the graduates of the University of Dublin, Trinity College. He is a member of the Foreign Affairs Committee of the Irish Parliament. Chairman of the James Joyce Centre, North Great Georges Street, and founding Chairman of the North Great Georges Street Preservation Society. He was awarded the gold and silver medals of the University Philosophical Society and the gold medal of the Brazilian Academy of Letters. He has written and broadcast widely in Europe and America on literary, political and sociological subjects. He successfully sued the Irish State in the European Court of Human Rights to secure the decriminalisation of male homosexual activity in Ireland.

"*What is truth?*" as jesting Pilate said. We might just as easily ask what is peace? For they are both in the words of Cap'n Boyle "*Daarlin, questions*". But like all abstract notions not all that easy to tie down. Well, I suppose we can be guided on our way by some of the usual clichés which at least have some residue of truth in them such as "*Peace is not just the absence of war*".

Perhaps we should start humbly with the individual rather than the community or nation. For even in a community that is outwardly peaceful there may be many individuals who for reasons of family tension, poverty, or problems in the work situation could scarcely be said to be personally experiencing peace as a condition. And if one is not at harmony with one's self, it is unlikely that one can extend the virtue of peace to ones neighbours. Moreover, what is true in the microcosm of individual life is also true of nations. A nation that is not at harmony with itself can scarcely be expected to be a peaceful neighbour. Germany and Russia in the 1930's or the two Korea's since the 1950's are representative examples of this fact.

When I think of peace I start from a religious angle although paradoxically one thing that drives me completely mad is the invasive new ritual of the 'sign of peace' engaged in nowadays by both the Roman Catholic and Anglican churches. The emotions this form of liturgical lapdancing releases in me are quite the reverse of peaceful. It seems a far cry from the beautiful language of the Vranmer Prayer Book with its Collect for Peace -

> *"Oh God, who art the author of peace and lover of concord, in knowledge of whom standeth our eternal life, whose service is perfect freedom; defend thy humble servants in all assaults of our enemies; that we, surely trust in thy defence, may not fear the power of any adversary; through the might of Jesus Christ Our Lord Amen"*

or that superbly calming and reassuring prayer -

> *"The Peace of God, which passeth all understanding, keep your hearts and minds and knowledge in the love of God".*

At a personal level I find peace in these prayers which have become like a mantra to me.

In the political sense I must own up to being an SRC - a State Registered Coward. I am old enough to remember the slogan *"Better Dead than Red"*. I never agreed with it. Most people even under the grim boot of tyranny retain sufficient of the chameleon effect to render the state of red as impermanent, whereas there is something dreadfully final about the state of being dead. And on the level of physical courage, an interrogator would only have to point a pincer at one of my toenails for me to divulge every secret of which I possessed and invent a few more for good measure.

That however did not deter me from becoming involved in the organisation of the Peace Train some years ago. This was a group that ran a gala train between Dublin and Belfast in defiance of IRA threats. This was done in order to highlight contradictions in Sinn Fein/IRA policy, for they claim as a principal objective the Unification of Ireland and it seemed to many of us bizarre that they should seek to bring about this objective by regularly blowing up the principal rail connection between Belfast and Dublin. Of course one of the things that entertained me ironically at the time was that as we sped between the two cities there was a constant outbreak of little spats and rivalries between the peace makers themselves while on their way to spread the joys of peace and harmony to others. Nevertheless it was a worthy and useful exercise.

I would like to think of myself as a pacifist, but of course there are contradictions here too. Everyone can indulge theoretically in notions of pacifism, but it is extremely difficult to restrain the human instinct to retaliate when a loved one is threatened. I recognise this but what is understandable for the individual is less so for the State. It is for this reason that I have consistently opposed the death penalty both here and abroad. There seems to me to be a distinct difference between a crime of passion or even a premeditated criminal murder on the one hand and allowing the State to sink to what is always the calculated destruction of the life of a citizen. Nor has the death penalty ever been proved to be an effective deterrent. It is simply revenge. And when, as one witnesses in the United States, the revenge of society is exacted disproportionately against the mentally weak, racial minorities and the poor, then surely this is a form of unjustifiable State violence.

Moreover, in traditional historical review, peace is sometimes used in an unintentionally ironic way. The Pax Romana of the ancient Empire was maintained by the might of the legions, the cruelty of gladiatorial display, while the Pax Britannica, its 19th century counterpart, was held in place by gunship diplomacy, the rigid enforcement of naval superiority and colonial domination. This moreover was resented by individual citizens. Even Edward VII - Edward the Peace Maker - came in for a few knocks in the lively conversation of James Joyce's Ulysses where the 'Citizen' shouts out that *"There's a lot more pox than pax about Edward Guelph-Wettin"*.

Of course sometimes it all depends on who the speaker is. Friends of mine in England treasure a cartoon showing a Trotskyite agitator of the 1960s addressing a group in Hyde Park, in a strong foreign accent and saying according to the caption underneath *"Vot ze English pipples vont is piss"*. In other words we may as a nation or an individual desire peace, but if we are lectured on this subject by those we perceive as outsiders, then the reaction is often contrariness and dismissal. On the subject of foreigners indeed one might well ask how peaceful do our current crop of immigrants, refugees and asylum seekers perceive this country to be. We are at peace with the world, we have a thriving economy and yet with shameful regularity people are abused, spat upon and even beaten up in the streets of Dublin simply because they are perceived as strangers to this country either because of their colour, their appearance or their accent.

On the political front I have tried to be active for peace, in particular engaging in critical reviews of the Amsterdam and Nice Treaties with a view to attempting to ensure that the State of Ireland is not walked imperceptibly into the arms of NATO without a full debate. I am also suspicious of what some of the European countries regard as 'peace'. The French Government for example described the infamous 'Operation Turquoise' as a peacekeeping mission even though it was, in effect, an intervention specifically designed to keep in place a known genocidal regime so that arms could be sold impartially all over the shop.

When at a Cossac meeting in Paris some years ago I attacked the French for their sale of Alouette helicopters and other war materials to the Indonesian regime which would be used against the unfortunate people of East Timor, the then French Foreign Minister Alain Juppé rebuked me saying that the European Union was not a humanitarian agency, that there were no human rights provision in the Union and that, in any case, it was a question of domestic concern involving employment. I am glad to say that one benefit of the Treaty of Amsterdam is that there is now increasingly human rights elements in the foundation treaties of the European Union. The argument towards employment in the munitions industry is, on the surface, an easy one for us in Ireland without an armament lobby to be high minded about. However, Afri have pointed to the fact that almost unknowingly some of our high tech industries are providing guidance systems and other technical elements for weapon systems so few, if any of us, can say that our hands are completely clean.

I remember arguing these points at a meeting a couple of years ago in the University of Limerick. I provoked the wrath of a distinguished professor from Wales who asked in heated tones what I would do if my mother was about to be raped by a Russian soldier. I replied that I could contemplate this event with equanimity as my mother had been dead for 33 years and I doubted if necrophilia, even in its most extreme form, would out last that period of interment, and in any case my answer would be roughly approximate to that of the late Lytton Strachey who when asked a similar question by a review board as a conscientious objector in the First World War replied *"I would attempt to interpose my own body"*. This reply in the light of Strachey's effeminacy was sufficiently ambiguous to daunt even the military interrogators.

There are times surveying the world scene when one is tempted to give in to despair. Sean McBride, Chief of Staff of the IRA, was given the Nobel Prize for Peace in between those two well known peace makers Henry Kissinger and Menachem Begin. This surely must call for redefinition of the word peace. Ariel Sharon was judged by an Israeli Commission after the Sabra and Chatilla massacres to be unfit to be Minister for Defence in the Israeli Government. Now he pops up as Prime Minister. His winning slogan in the election was *"Ain Shalom Bli Biticon"* - No Peace without Security. A better slogan would have been *"Ain Shalom Mi Sharon"* - No Peace with Sharon". He promised an end to attacks on civilians and yet they have multiplied steadily since his election. He, like many strong men of politics throughout the world with a military background, appears to believe that violence should be met by greater violence. However most people see this as leading to an unending cycle of greater devastation all round.

There is perhaps one beacon of hope among world leaders and that is the solitary figure of the Dalai Lama. For fifty years he has trod the lonely path of peace in international affairs. And his reward? To be marginalised by leaders of the world community though not its peoples. It was a most disgraceful thing last autumn when the UN organised a meeting of world spiritual leaders committed to peace and at the behest of the atheistic Chinese regime pointedly excluded the Dalai Lama. However he appears indefatigable. I recall spending an hour with him in Dharamsalla after a secret visit to Tibet. He told me that he was praying for the Chinese because he was afraid that they were damaging their souls by their violence against his people. If only we could all aspire to such a noble notion of peace.

There is no way to peace. Peace is the way.

A. J. Muste

The Idea and Process of Peace

James O'Connell

Dr. James O'Connell is a Professor Emeritus of Peace Studies at the
University of Bradford. He holds a Master of Arts from NUI and a
Ph.D from Louvain. He has worked in the University of Ibadan,
Nigeria, Ahmadu Bello University, University of Warwick, and
Northern Ireland Polytechnic. He has published many books and
papers on peace, ethnicity, epistemology, metaphysics, and theology.

The search for peace has been a perennial task in human history. In
our times peace has become more critical than ever before: the
shadow of nuclear destruction is going to hang ominously over the
foreseeable future: and the nuclear threat is compounded by advances in
biological and chemical weapons. Yet that same technology, out of which
weapons of mass destruction have come, makes the world grow small in
production, trade and communications. The new global closeness
emphasizes the functional interdependence of the world's regions; it
increases awareness of comparative living conditions; and it sharpens
competition for global resources between states as well as deepening ethnic
and class cleavages within states.

Against this background let me describe broadly the idea and process of
peace. Peace is - in St. Augustine's great definition – *"the tranquillity of order"*
(City of God: XIX:13). It has a positive and a negative dimension.
Positively, peace requires co-operation among persons and groups for aims
that include security, justice and freedom; and, negatively, it envisages the
absence of force and violence. In the positive dimension of peace each aim
is important: security guarantees survival; justice underpins the links of

social co-operation without which peace remains fragile; and freedom, finally, gives worth to persons who otherwise in being unable to choose their own future would remain diminished. The negative dimension of peace - the absence of violence - in its turn is necessary for letting people get on with their lives without disruption.

The process of peace means that peace has to be sought through the efforts of individuals and groups; it has to be worked on and maintained; and where it has been broken it needs to be restored through social re-structuring and mediation, through forgiveness and reconciliation. In a profound sense if peace is the end, it is also the means to the end. For that reason involved in a living understanding of peace is a set of attitudes among persons and groups that are dynamic and purposeful and that seek to uphold the values of security, justice and freedom inherent in stabilising peace. In short, peace has to be all the time worked for.

History suggests that during or leading up to conflict, groups with opposing interests develop mutually unfavourable images of, and make adverse judgements on, one another. There are three factors underlying such perceptions/judgements – competition (interest–conflict-intensity), communication or lack of it, and confidence. All three are conditioned by the history and organisation of the disputants, the values they hold, and the sentiments they cherish. In this context, converging or compatible interests, socio-political structures capable of being used to control or mediate situations of potential conflict of interests, and mechanisms for maintaining communication and creating confidence are essential to dealing with conflict.

It is difficult to resolve conflict where there is a substantial clash of interests between opposing groups, that is to say, where one group - or two or more groups in conflict - has to renounce substantial advantages. The only way to deal with this problem is to convince groups that they will benefit from compromise in the longer run and that all groups grow through co-operation, understanding and generosity.

For dealing with conflict, accommodation which is conciliation in the widest sense is indispensable: a process that takes in honest negotiations, rethinking and reworking aims, and reciprocated concessions. Accommodation is however often bedeviled by the misunderstanding of conciliation. What is for some conciliation is readily presented by others as appeasement. In Northern Irish negotiations hard-line unionists have consistently argued that they have had to make concessions while receiving little in return from nationalists, while hard-line nationalists have argued that unionists have made no concessions that they have not been forced into.

Within countries, and in relations between countries, it is necessary to have social and political structures (bi-lateral/multi-lateral) that are capable of integrating technology, serving interests and containing competition. The original fault in creating Northern Ireland was to take in counties and territories that made Protestant hegemony precarious and prepared the way for insecurity and discrimination, and eventually, rebellion. It took two bitter European civil wars before Western European powers discovered that their economies converged and that while they were likely to go on being in tension with one another, they could be contained within new politico-economic structures.   Out of this understanding came the

European Economic Community in 1958 which was created only thirteen years after the end of the 1939-45 war.

Finally, in talking about rendering interests compatible, elaborating integrative political structures and maintaining communication and confidence, it is important not to concentrate on solutions only. It is indispensable to get warring sides to the table, but if they do come to the table and reach an initial agreement, it is even more important to maintain the momentum gained: as people try to work out inadequate but acceptable forms of accommodation they change gradually longer term and intractable problems. In other words, instead of demanding solutions where there are none, sensible efforts and phasing can manage to reach a minimally acceptable accommodation and in the process enable longer-term problems to take on new and more benign shapes. Politics consists in finding immediate answers to problems that are ultimately unsolvable. In other words, politics is process rather than solution.

Ours is a world where we will live together or die together. The process of peace is the crucial condition for sharing our global world as well as its regional parts. Through peace we can make proper use of our technology, seek to share justly the world's goods among its peoples and regions, and enter into those dialogues among cultures through which we grow in knowledge, mutual aid and artistic achievement.

Nelson

Maria O'Dwyer

Maria O'Dwyer is a PhD candidate at the Centre for Peace and Development Studies, University of Limerick.

Nelson stared staidly into his coffee as George once again harassed the young waiter about introducing a new menu, 'one which wouldn't cater for just one type of person, but one which would offer something acceptable to all'. The waiter poured a fresh carafe of water and as the sound echoed through Nelson's mind he cast his thoughts to the floods in Mozambique. From under a carefully folded napkin, a steak knife peeked out. In Nelson's mind it seemed to represent the epitome of man's inhumanity to his fellow man. He shuffled restlessly in his seat. Brother fighting brother. Neighbours who become enemies in the same war. Children being exposed to prejudices and hatred. A world ravaged by the kind of intolerance that breed's separatism, which in its turn breeds extremism, until the cycle starts all over again. A hearty laugh from his lunch partner harnessed his straying thoughts. *"Tell me my friend"*, Nelson asked in a fatigued tone *"what do you think this agreement will do for the people in Northern Ireland"*.

"If I learned one thing from all of this Nelson, it is that any attempt at explanation is likely to be considered partial. We're talking about propaganda wars – if you give to Peter, you're automatically perceived as having taken from Paul. Majority-minority situations offer themselves as breeding-grounds for suspicion, where groups watch each other with the kind of arched eyebrows that typify mistrust. For many of the people in

Northern Ireland the Agreement is little more than a political chessboard, with words such as 'multi-party negotiation', 'historic opportunity', 'equality', 'mutual respect' and so forth being used as the pawns. For a lot of others, it offers a fresh hope in a situation that has been considered stale for such a long time. Perhaps the best way to explain the situation to you my friend would be to borrow a phrase used in the framework for agreement: There are deep divisions between the members of the two traditions living there over their respective senses of identity and allegiance, their views on the present status of Northern Ireland and their vision of future relationships in Ireland and between the two islands."

Again Nelson allowed himself to escape into the privacy of his own thoughts. Mankind's track record demonstrates its unerring ability to create boundaries of separation. Though he had always been well read on the situation in Northern Ireland, the 'Troubles' had never failed to confound him. Mutual mistrust reinforced a barrier of fear and hatred. He saw an internal conflict, where one group needed to be demonised in order to make a martyr's cause of the other.

George thought back to his time in Ireland. He also pondered for a moment on the long and turbulent history of Anglo-Irish relations and the agreement he was endeavouring to explain to his colleague. Indeed, he himself was unsure of the changes, however slight, which the agreement would bring. He considered the whole constitutional/political debate. It appeared to go without saying that a political settlement in Northern Ireland is a forerunner to the establishment of any lasting peace, yet every advance seemed to have had a corresponding step back, just as every new hope was shadowed by the reminiscence of a past failure. He remembered being briefed about a power sharing executive way back in 1973. That had been an agreed political settlement but, in essence, what had it achieved? George thought about the historical and cultural cleavages, the sectarian hatred that inspired so much violence and loss, and the tide of suspicion that had for so long come in over the shores of Northern Ireland. What would a post-agreement North look like?

Leaving the restaurant, the noises of the lunchtime city were drowned out by the sounds of the bands marching in George's head. The familiar tunes of the Orangemen were stored subliminally somewhere at the back of his mind, as were the haunting laments of the republicans. As the image of a green shamrock attached to an orange sash flashed through his mind, George took his colleague by the arm. *"You know, Mandela"*, he said in a triumphant tone, *"we will judge the success of the agreement by the falling of the arched eyebrow"*.

All must love the human form,
In heathen, Turk, or Jew;
Where Mercy, Love, and Pity dwell
There God is dwelling too.

William Blake

Peace and the Healing of Ireland:
A Christian Perspective
Paul O'Higgins

Paul O'Higgins is an ordained Christian Minister and the Director of Reconciliation Outreach. He is a native of Ireland now residing in Stuart, Florida, and holds a doctorate in Biblical Theology. Together with his wife Nuala he has written several books, including 'Christianity without Religion', 'The Healing of Ireland', 'In Israel Today with Jesus' and 'The Tree of Life'. The O'Higgins have travelled to over 25 countries, in an interdenominational ministry of teaching and reconciliation. He ministers extensively throughout Ireland each year.

C an a nation be healed? Is it possible for a people to recover from the anguish and pain of their past; or is history a ball and chain to be carried by the present generation into its emerging future?

At the threshold of a new millennium, Ireland stands with one hand reaching towards a golden age of peace and opportunity, and the other hand chained to the hurts of our past. A courageous new generation is emerging in Ireland determined to break with the mistakes of the past. They are creating a New Ireland moving to possess its opportunities and overcome the handicaps of history. Will we succeed in this and sweep away the senseless inherited hatreds or will the memories and voices of our past shackle us to ancient patterns of hostility?

Political and economic advances over the last few years have created new opportunities in Ireland. Yet for all this welcome progress we have in Northern Ireland a society that remains segregated and filled with sectarian tension and violence. Political arrangements have their part to play in the healing process but they can only succeed when they reflect a genuine change in the prevailing attitudes of our people. Swiss theologian Hans Kung remarked that *"the most fanatical and cruelest political struggles are those that have been coloured, inspired and legitimised by religion"*. If this is true any consideration of the healing of Ireland must address the underlying religious sentiments of Irish society.

Does Christianity itself have anything to bring to the quest for peace in Ireland today? By Christianity we do not mean the petty rivalry between churches, but the teachings of Jesus and the new realities set in place by his death and resurrection.

The teaching and work of Jesus set in motion a revolutionary new approach to peace making: Peace through forgiveness.

The Christian teaching is that peace can only be

- attained through forgiveness and
- maintained by forgiveness.

It is not simply that those who have been wronged extend forgiveness to those who have wronged them; but they also realise that they too stand in need of forgiveness. There is consequently no boasting of the one over the other; no claim that I am the 'good' person and you are the 'bad' person.

When I extend forgiveness to the one who has injured me, treated me unjustly, despised me or deprived me of my rights, I do so knowing that I share the same humanity as the one I forgive. My task is not so much to deal with the 'speck' in my neighbour's eye, but to remove the 'log' in my eye, which causes me to be irritated by my neighbour in the first place.

As long as we remain locked in the historic and tribal position of defending 'our' side and pointing the finger at the 'other side' there can be no escape from the impasse of alienation. The Christian challenge is to remove from our own lives behaviors, words and actions that destroy harmony and create hostility. Jesus gave His followers a revolutionary commandment: *"Love one another as I have loved you"*. He required them to love those they have been conditioned to regard as enemies.

The Christian is called to deliberately put away negative actions and attitudes and he and 'his side' (whichever that side may be) have towards people of the 'other side'. To attain lasting peace in our land we need to recognise, renounce, reject and cut off patterns of hostility which we have inbibed from our culture or tradition. We have to recognise the sins of our ancestors and deliberately break with them. We do this by:

- facing up to the inherited sins and prejudices of our fathers,
- breaking with them as they influence us,
- receiving God's forgiveness for them (fully available to all through the atoning sacrifice of Jesus) and
- receiving the power of the Holy Spirit to move beyond them.

Our education and religious systems programmed us to see our nation in terms of 'good guys' and 'bad guys'. As a child growing up in Limerick my 'good guys' were the Unionists' 'bad guys' and their 'good guys' were my 'bad guys'. Of course 'our side' was the 'good side' and theirs was the 'bad side' and *vice versa*. One of the tasks of true Christianity is to help us break with such biased patterns of belief. True Christianity tells me that there is an evil within me, which if left unchecked can cause me to hurt those around me. It tells me that my primary task is to deal with this evil and then to forgive the evil I see in the other. It enables me to see that our side (whichever it is) has no monopoly on good and no immunity from evil. It tells me that it is more important for me to reject the evil I see within myself, than to condemn the evil in those around me.

The challenge to this generation of Irish people is:

- whether we will perpetuate the hatreds and tribalism of the past or recognise them as wrong;
- whether we will endlessly revisit the injustices of the past or give and receive forgiveness for these wrongs.

The challenge of every Nationalist and Unionist is not necessarily to renounce their political and religious ideologies, but to recognise and refuse any inbuilt hatred, prejudice or hostility they receive with their political and religious preferences.

As in His days on earth, religious labels and parties do not impress Jesus. He calls people from every background to transcend the limitations of their culture and follow Him and His example to love our 'enemies' (real or perceived) as well as our friends. Today we see many Irish people moving beyond the shadows of religion and politics into the full light and peace of the kingdom of God. His word for us at this time in our history is *"Friends come up higher!"* The invitation is His; the choice is ours.

The Harvest of Peace

Brendan O'Regan

Brendan O'Regan is a former Chairman of Shannon Development; Bord Fáilte; and DEVCO (State Agencies Development Co-operation Organisation). He is Founder and President of Co-operation Ireland and the Centre for International Co-operation; Founder and Patron of the Irish Peace Institute; and Founder Member of Obair (Newmarket-on-Fergus). He is a recipient of the Paul Harris Award and the C.B.E., for promoting peace through understanding. He was awarded an Honorary Doctorate in Law by the National University of Ireland (NUI) in 1978. A similar award was made to him in 1999 by Queens University Belfast and in 2001 by the University of Limerick, to mark his work for peace. He is a Freeman of the City of Limerick.

We have had thirty years experience of what is euphemistically called 'the troubles'. In that time we have learnt at least two things: that there is no easy political solution to this problem and that 90% of people on both sides want to live out their lives in peace, harmony and prosperity.

What I am writing very simply is that the time to harness the fire is right now. Forty-four years ago on the 25th of March 1957 Europe, the most strife-torn landmass on our planet, sown with more blood, hatred and bitterness than fire has ever generated in recorded history, decided to opt for cultivation and progress rather than destruction. Thus, the European Economic Community was founded and eventually grew to become what we now know as the European Union. However, it did not begin as a united political Europe, it was a fragile bond of continual dialogue lasting, frequently, into the early hours of the morning. But it did work and, more importantly, it healed those wounds between Germans, Belgians, French,

207

British, Dutch and Italians. The transformation was achieved by skilfully managed, large scale co-operation.

My one suggestion in this essay is that such a transformation is possible for us. The machinery is there, the funds are there, the expertise and experience are there. And we are the only ones who are not yet there. I myself have had experience of managed co-operation on a much smaller scale, between Northern Ireland and the Republic of Ireland, before the troubles. I saw then the possibilities of a similar transformation on this island. At the time, I was appointed Chairman of Bord Fáilte and of the Shannon Free Airport Development Company and had the privilege of watching the emergence of Shannon Airport, a new town and an international industrial zone, from a fairly unpromising area of unused land. Both these developments were the result of organised co-operation, committed endeavour and imaginative professional use of funds.

Without wasting precious time or going into too much detail, I must sketch for you the possibilities which exist now for both our communities to achieve a similar kind of co-operative growth which will be mutually beneficial without being individually compromising. Before I do, let me tell you this: the cost of one days violence on this island is greater than any monies which have been allocated in a year to such organised endeavours as I have in mind, that is - skilfully managed co-operation pursuing a policy of active good neighbourliness; to harness the fire and to transform the present situation. I am not talking about pious sentiment or political promise, I am talking about hard-nosed realism and investment for the future.

Funds are at this moment available and adequate for this task and I am making a plea for support for bodies working to achieve understanding and co-operation in this island.

But, I am pleading particularly for skilfully managed and experienced organisations that have a track record of promoting co-operation across borders. Inclusive non-governmental, cross-border organisations have developed to the stage at which they can and should be used as a way forward for all people in Northern Ireland and the Republic of Ireland. Their importance in the history of conflict comes from what they have done, what they are doing and, most important of all, what they could do in the future to promote widespread good neighbourliness, understanding and co-operation between North and South.

Our experience in Ireland provides the blueprint for the promotion of peace. Cross-border structures can be effective in managing and promoting contact however, that contact needs to be focused and directed to achieve the maximum benefit. A division of labour between the various organisations should exist and our experience can provide a template for effective synergy of peace-keeping.

Wherever human conflict exists the way forward can be found through co-operation and I am sure that with God's help, co-operation in Ireland and internationally, will reap tomorrow the harvest of economic stability and peace. The harvest will be reaped and the fire harnessed by increased co-operation.

Co-operation Ireland, the Irish Peace Institute, and similar peace-building organisations are promoted and accepted because they are non-political and have no prejudice or proselytising intent. Their aim is to overcome violence and unemployment through an increasing scale of economic, cultural and social co-operation between Northern Ireland and the Republic of Ireland. There now exists the most elaborate network of co-operation between the people of Northern Ireland and the Republic of Ireland, in almost every sphere of activity. The indispensable network of co-operation in Ireland has laid the groundwork for the kind of socio-economic links which could strengthen the current economic buoyancy. There are over twenty years of trusted experience on both sides of the border which has paved all the groundwork and dug the canals. All it needs now is the sluice gates to open and the funds to pour in.

These organisations, created to co-ordinate programmes on a local scale, have an important role to play in promoting educational developments based on that practical experience and spreading the message of co-operation both locally and globally. The importance of promoting this fact internationally relates directly to the urgent task of creating jobs in Ireland - North and South. More tourism and industrial investment will be quickly attracted when (despite our political differences) we are seen to be engaged in a large scale programme of economic and social co-operation on this island as a focus for international co-operation and peace-building. Its credibility rests upon the successful example of Co-operation Ireland's formula which is non-governmental and that of other peace-building organisations in the island of Ireland.

When commercial enterprises begin to see this process as part of their professional portfolio, and that managed co-operation pays, then vast untapped forces are unleashed. Managed co-operation opens the way to peace now.

The funds exist, the formula exists, all we need is to harness the fire right now and reap the benefits of peace on a global scale.

Peace is certain. It is not only a matter of time... In this case as in other fields nothing in the universe can resist the converging energies of a sufficient number of minds sufficiently grouped and organised.

Teilhard de Chardin

Abba Father
Mícheál Ó Súilleabháin

Mícheál Ó Súilleabháin, Composer, Musicologist and Performer is currently Professor of Music at the University of Limerick. Prior to his recent appointment to the University of Limerick, he lectured in University College Cork.

Abba Father
wholesome name
earth and heavan
be the same.

Teach us now
to be forgiving,
to be trusting
in our living.

As You forgive
our darkest night
that we may live
within Your light

Do not lead us
towards temptation.
Lead us towards
a sound salvation.

Through your kingdom's
glorious power
our hearts and minds
and souls will flower.

Abba Father
once again
show us love and peace.
Amen.

Return to me
(after St. Francis' prayer)

Lord, make me your peace path.

Hatred lives not in the fields of love
and where the heart lies broken, forgiving mists will rise,
discord turn its head towards beauty
and seeds find fertile fruit in opened ground.

Despair! Give way to hope,
and sadness, joy,
and where darkness lies within the frightened fog
Let there be light

Consolation of my soul
Understanding of my mind
Heartlove of my breast
Return to me

Rising hand's gift
Return to me.

Blessed hand's hope
Return to me.

Seeded darkness without sight
Journey through the soul's dark night
Breaking ground, revealing light
Return to me

Eternal flame of wholesome love
Return to me

Amen

Inner Peace

Colin Parry

The Warrington bombing was a key point in the IRA's mainland bombing campaign, which shifted the focus of violence away from the province. But it also led Colin Parry, Tim's father, to launch himself into a highly public campaign for peace both in the UK, Ireland and the USA. He has since won praise from both UK and Irish leaders for his determined efforts to ensure his son did not die in vain. On the seventh anniversary of the fatal bomb blast, in March this year, as a result of the tireless campaigning and fund-raising of Colin and Wendy Parry, a £3m peace centre for young people was opened in Warrington. They helped set up a peace initiative within months of the explosion and have said that the Tim Parry - Jonathan Ball Young People's Centre is the realisation of their dreams and will be a safe haven for children.

When my son Tim was killed by an act of barbarity committed by a fellow human being in the name of his ancient cause, my life, and that of his mother and his older brother and his younger sister, his grandparents, cousins and his wider family and his close friends, were changed...forever.

Tim was taken at the age of twelve. Another young boy of three was killed too. Fifty six other people were injured and countless hundreds were terrified and experienced a life changing event.

I lay on Tim's bed in the moments before he died; I held him close to me for the final time; I kissed him and told him how much I loved him and that I would look forward to the day we could be together again. I stayed to hold his hand when his life support machine was switched off; I did not want him to slip into the next world without me there to guide him.

My final time with Tim was when I sat with him in the chapel of rest at the funeral parlour. He was stone cold; his face was only partly uncovered; we had never seen the horrific injuries he had sustained to his beautiful face; it was to stay this way even in the final moments. My son lay dead and yet I still talked to him - it was strangely reassuring to do so. Leaving that quiet, still room was so hard because it was so final. Days later, Tim's older brother Dominic, helped me to carry Tim's coffin and lay him to rest in the ground. I was very proud of my other son. My daughter Abigail dropped Tim's Everton Football Club teddy bear in to the grave. We said our farewells and we felt our private thoughts. For me, it was how will life go on without him?

One of the least expected, yet most uplifting things to happen after the IRA bombed Warrington, was the massive number of loving letters from Ireland we received. Yes there were more from around Britain, but relative to the populations, we received a disproportionately large number from Ireland, north and south of the border.

Complete strangers poured their hearts out to us, but so many also implored me to continue to speak out - as a father. So, I did and it is through the simple act of talking to people that I came to understand that I could make a contribution to peace and reconciliation. Ironically, my career has always been in the people business, as a Human Resources professional in industry. Yet despite knowing I was a capable enough communicator, often on complex business matters, I had to accept I had no experience of discussing deeply personal matters, and certainly not with strangers. Neither had I any experience of dealing with the media; but I learned fast, and through these twin media I was able to deliver my story, or to be more accurate, Tim's story, to millions through a TV screen and to tens, hundreds and occasionally thousands through personal appearances.

All of this cemented my growing belief in the power of story telling as a way of influencing others. People listened to me and questioned me and from my perspective of not representing any one or anything, other than myself and my family, I was never constrained from telling it as it was. Honesty and truth are sometimes far removed from the priorities of people tied to an organisational message - I had no such worries.

My sense of inner peace grew from telling Tim's and Tim's family's story. Undoubtedly, it gained me the backing of influential people and, through this, I was able to establish The Tim Parry - Jonathan Ball Trust, a charity pledged to help young people deal with the consequences of intolerance, prejudice, and inter-community violence.

In turn, we were able to build The Tim Parry - Jonathan Ball Young People's Centre, otherwise more simply known as the 'Peace Centre' in Warrington. It provides a brilliant and safe venue for young people to come together in a spirit of friendship and tolerance. People from all over the world have already visited and stayed in the Peace Centre within the first ten months of being open.

We have introduced a campaign in the name, 'Children for Peace'. The campaign marks the start of creating programmes of learning to meet the needs of all young people regardless of their age, race, religion, politics, nationality or anything else that may be used as an excuse for prejudice or violence.

In Tim's and Jonathan's memory, the Trust and the Peace Centre will carry their names as constant reminders of the terribly high cost paid when too few human beings care enough to try and make a difference.

I fully accept that I was one of those human beings who lived his own selfish life without any sense that I could and should try to make a difference. Tim's death robbed me of a beloved and beautiful child; it also compelled me to reach out and work for peace and reconciliation… had I not done so, it would have been a betrayal of my son. He would not have expected me to do anything else but do my best and through that, find inner peace.

Mission of Peace

Michael Shannon

Michael Shannon is a retired Colonel who served with UN forces in numerous peace-keeping operations. He is the Chairman of the Irish Peace Institute based at the University of Limerick, Plassey.

I n 1978 I was serving with the 44th Irish Infantry Battalion deployed on peace-keeping duties with the United Nations Interim Force in Lebanon (UNIFIL). Seven hundred and fifty Irishmen were engaged with soldiers from many other nations in implementing the most difficult task of keeping the peace in Lebanon. As an officer in mid-career, who had served on many other missions for peace, I remember coming to the conclusion that despite all the bombardments, rocket and mortar fire, not to mention small arms fire, that conflict is not inevitable, but to achieve this, the need is great to put prevention of deadly conflict at the highest place in the world's collective endeavours. The main reason that we hear and see recurring violence on our television screens is that we have not applied our minds to ensure we act speedily and skilfully with all the diplomatic, political, economic and military resources available to us. Very often violence and conflict reach massive proportions before we begin to take action to defuse these incidents of deadly violence.

> Peace, the very antithesis of war, is, or should be, the abiding responsibility of leaders of governments and non-governmental institutions. There are no dividends to be gained from strife, conflict or deadly warfare to mankind, or indeed to the actual combatants themselves, either in the short term or long term of any conflicts around the globe.

"You bring me the greatest joy that can be felt by a man whose invincible belief is that science and peace will triumph over ignorance and war, that nations will unite, not to destroy, but to build, and that the future will belong to those who will have done the most for suffering humanity."

Thus spoke Louis Pastéur at the University of the Sorbonne in Paris in 1892. Pastéur's words did not come to pass in the twentieth century, but those of us who believe in them must never despair in working towards bringing Pastéur's dream to fruition in this new century of education, peace-keeping and the obvious goal of most of the world's governments attempting to attain peace. Since wars begin in the minds of men, it is in the minds of men that the defences of peace must be constructed.

I have seen many dedicated soldiers, diplomats and politicians display extraordinary commitment to peace and a refusal to believe that war and conflict cannot be prevented in our time. Some of these soldiers serving in the honourable cause of peace and conflict resolution have lost their lives because of the actions of certain states, who are incidentally members of the United Nations, and who have deliberately ignored the mandate of the U.N., because their national policies conflicted with the desires of the U.N..

It is my firm ingrained belief that the coming together of nations in this new century, to control the arms race, to prevent conflict and stop the devastation of war by preventative measures of peace-keeping, will usher in an era of true peace.

Nations must engage in training more troops and civilians, in advance of anticipated conflict, in the tactics, techniques and science of peace-keeping.

They must fine tune their foreign policies and diplomatic skills to prevent a drift away from peace in any threatening situation. The cost of this type of preparedness is only a fraction of the cost of a small localised conflict in any part of the globe.

Ireland has a proud record, since 1958, of active dedication to peace-keeping in many countries all over the world. We, as a small country, must redouble our efforts to provide military personnel in conjunction with civilian agencies, to go out and continue our peacekeeping policies. We must not fail the cause of keeping the peace. The Irish people have given massive support to this noble policy over the years. I have been privileged to be part of this great humanitarian crusade in over twenty countries. We do not want to see countries like Angola, Bosnia, Kosovo, Lebanon, etc., devastated by savage warfare.

We cannot fail in our mission of peace. We must not fail. *"There never was a bad peace and there never was a good war".*

Who ever could make two ears of corn or two blades of grass to grow upon a spot of ground where only one grew before, would deserve better of mankind, and do more essential service to his country than the whole race of politicians put together.

Jonathan Swift

From a Grudge Culture
to a Growth Culture
Noel Stephen Flannery

Noel Stephen Flannery is a lecturer in economics. He is also involved in the business sector and is a member of Limerick's Philosophical Society. He lived for some time abroad.

P eace is easier when closed societies are transformed to open societies. An open society is inclusive, non threatening and with parity of esteem, non insulting. Diversity is seen as a resource by a creative community. An open society is based on an ideology of liberty rather than race or culture. Knowledge is the source of growth. Karl Popper, father of an open society, saw all knowledge as evolving in a process of research and theory so new ideas are welcome and criticism is invited. Pluralism and tolerance are the norm, so all forms of thinking are allowed but no form of thuggery. The paradox of a tolerant society is in order to survive it must be intolerant of undemocratic groups like fascists, communists, ultra-nationalists or fundamentalist religious parties. Society must be vigilant against all paramilitary political parties as they would hinder or abolish free elections.

Modern republics are open societies. You are free to be different in a republic. The Latin word is *res publica*, thing of the people, meaning people are sovereign and all else is a thing. A modern republic is a democracy where all power comes from the people and the people are the measure of everything. Nothing is predetermined, only the people are sacred and they can change their minds as often as they like. Nothing is ruled out for consideration and debate. The dead generations or dead philosophies have no veto on the will of the people. The present can learn from the past but in no way are the people hostages to history.

John Locke influenced the craftsmen of the U.S.A. constitution forged on the anvil of the Dissenter religion. A republic is neutral on culture and maximises individual freedom. Privilege is replaced by equality before the law, monarchy by democracy and aristocracy by meritocracy. Only man has inalienable rights and the goal of society is to preserve these rights. The government belongs to the people, not the people belonging to the government. The people can cut the government to any size or shape they desire. John Locke wrote:

> *"government existed because men agreed with other men to join or unite into a community for their comfortable, safe and peaceable living one amongst another. In return for security provided, every man consenting with others to form one body politic under one government, puts himself under an obligation to every one of that society to submit to the determination of the majority. In submitting to government the only rights man gave up were those necessary for the regulation and preservation of property, the defence of the community and for the common good of the community. The relationship between citizen and government was a social contract and the rights of government came from the people in that contract".*

A constitution therefore is a social contract between the people to be governed and the government. A constitution should contain only fundamental principles and as few as possible so that minorities as well as the majority can agree to it. Confining a constitution to democratic rights, UN human rights and what Americans call *"self evident truths"* will make it inclusive. If the religious beliefs or culture of the majority are enshrined in it, then it is exclusive. Anything contentious should be left to legislation. The acid test of any democracy is how minorities are treated. Thomas Jefferson rejoiced over the success of Jews in the U.S.A. as it demonstrated the quality of liberty delivered by the American constitution.

Power corrupts and absolute power corrupts absolutely. Locke's idea was that the legislative and executive power of the government should be in different hands and that the judiciary should be independent to interpret the law. These checks and balances are to ensure the rule of law, prevent big governments stealing the rights of man and that the people can freely elect or remove the government. The purpose of government is to maximise the happiness of the people; that means treating all the people as well as possible. Anti-statism is part of American Republicanism; the state interferes as little as possible in people's lives and only creates the conditions for democratic and economic freedom, the people provide for themselves. Social engineering or a culture requiring compulsory conformity is not liberty.

Open societies are the most peaceful, prosperous societies in the world due to free trade in products and ideas. Open minds and open markets maximise innovation when a growth seeking culture replaces a conflict seeking culture. International trade has replaced war and you win in the market place by producing a greater flow of goods at prices that are better value for money. The only way this can be done is by increasing knowledge and this brings a mutual gain to all. Successful cultures esteem the person for their research and creative skills. Economics of self-sufficiency produce stagnation and poverty and integration maximises real wages. Economic integration removes borders, makes us all brothers and changed Ireland from an isolated island to an intelligent island.

The irony of open societies with individual freedom is that certain cultures acting voluntarily from a good community spirit and skilled at forming strong relationships, do best. Such groups are the Quakers, Jews, Irish (Fourteen Presidents of the U.S.A. and two Prime Ministers of the U.K. were Irish). Their converged culture stresses mastery rather than dependency, serving your fellow man by good deeds is the way to God and as such work is a prayer. God will judge not by your race or religion but by the good deeds you do. Honesty and truth builds a good community and a profitable firm. Long term the profit of a firm comes not from cheating but from strong relationships with it's customers and between the firm and it's workers. It is a coalition that can be destroyed by any group maximising their share at the expense of the other groups. Compromise and a fair division will strengthen the coalition. It's values are universal and in practise, long term these values benefit all.

Building good communities that are well bonded and in which the individual flourishes is compared to building a wall. A stone wall is good and a brick wall bad. A stone wall is an open society as each stone gets the minimum shaping for it to fit in. The builder is slower and requires much more skill at getting a strong structure where all the component parts are different. A strong cement is used to bind it together and bigger stones are selected for the outside to support the smaller stones in the middle. Corner stones are special as in the Bible *"the stone which the builders rejected has become the corner stone".* In the context of peace, special indeed are the persons who link different communities together. An open society is a family of communities; orange to green and all shades in between. There are over sixty different religious faiths in Ireland. In work the law of comparative advantage applies where the skills and personality are matched with the job to be done. Synergy is where the total is greater than the sum of the parts as cultures converge and individual gifts complement each other. In pre-mechanised farming men did the heavy field work and women did the house work and lighter work. Women were better at rearing young animals. Modern firms now recognise that women relatively are better at communication and networking. Work is more a social place and women are more interested in people and know a lot about each other. If a worker's child is injured they can ask is it Jenny or Jack? A woman's perspective is important on the design of a product to satisfy customers' demands and the structure of a firm to satisfy workers needs.

A brick wall represents a closed society as all the bricks are identical. To be accepted into a closed society uniformity is required, so a person becomes homogenised. *"Why can't a woman be more like a man?"* sings Henry Higgins. You are not a real Irishman unless you have an O or a Mac in front of your name says the ultra-nationalist and even if you have Gaelic genes you will be deemed unfit to be a citizen of his republic unless you agree one hundred percent with him. An Irish rugby team beat England early in the last century to much acclaim, but the fanatics said that's no Irish team, there are fourteen Protestants and one Jew on that team. In high society of My

Fair's Lady's time, elocution, etiquette and clothes were very important to a lady. The flower girl was taken apart and reconstructed in order to fit into society. The strength of a closed society depends on uniformity and the method of construction is easier and quicker but the innate talents of the individuals are lost in the shaping. Bureaucrats love this design, a case of the bland leading the blind. Too much structure leads to stagnation and a pyramid power increases dependency.

Peace for me comes when an open society neither controls nor shapes individuals. Social engineering is low key and nothing is predetermined in order to be flexible and to maximise the freedom to choose. It accommodates diversity and builds a structure that utilises the strengths that different gifts can provide. A combination of orange and green is much more creative than two polarised societies. I am Mr. Bits as are most people; I am Irish born, but a grandfather was foreign. My culture is bits of Irish, British, American and elsewhere; a culture of accretion, overlay, bits of this and that. As Robert Burns wrote, *"a Man's a Man for a' that"*. Social mobility within a society creates natural bonding where individuals are helped to reach her/his potential.

Status is based on being self-made and earned achievement. Success depends on mutual 'use' of each other so that with the benefits of synergy and organisations we can achieve more in bigger units. Sick is the system where leaders can gain status by abusing others for personal ends or society's ends. A glorious short term ending can be used to justify violence. Violent macho men pushing to the top, rather than brains promoted to the top, will have long term consequences of internal repression and economic disaster. The long term ending may not be so glorious as Hitler, Stalin, and Franco were to prove. Europe united by persuasion will be a far better place than Europe united by force as Napoleon tried. The humane use of human beings has triumphed, bringing peace and prosperity in the liberal inclusive democracies of the West. Treated fairly, people are peaceful and for a pluralist people that means an open society. My Fair Lady summed it up; it is not how you dress or speak that makes you a lady, *it is how you are treated.*

We must organize our civilization and our collective action for the sake of peace.

Jean Monnet

The Enemy of Peace
Barbara Sweetman FitzGerald

> *Barbara Sweetman FitzGerald worked for the Irish Association for twelve years. She is on the executive committee of the British-Irish Association, a member of the Advisory Committee of the Ireland Funds and a board member of Oxfam Ireland. She is also involved with the Glenstal Ecumenical Conference.*

On being asked to write about Peace my first reaction was to think of Northern Ireland and the work I have been involved in since 1987 with The Irish Association, the oldest north/south body working in the field of peace and reconciliation. But then I started to think of what Peace really means to me and, at the risk of being personal, thought I would write about it.

Since returning from New York in 1963, my husband Michael and I became increasingly interested in what was happening in Northern Ireland. In a small way we did what we could to help, mainly by getting to know and understand the situation through friends and contacts.

Then Michael got involved in Ireland's entry in to what was then the European Economic Community. After a successful campaign, Ireland voted to join Europe, and a group of businessmen travelled to Brussels for a further meeting. We drove Michael to the airport and then I took our six children to play on the swings in a park while they discussed what present to give him for his birthday in ten days time, when he would have been thirty-seven. On arriving home, the children went to play, and I went to lie down for a while. As I lay, I suddenly felt the most amazing sense of Peace. I had never had such an experience before and marvelled at it. When one of the children came to tell me there had been an air crash in London, I said not to worry, as Daddy had flown direct to Brussels. Dublin airport was in transition in those days and I did not know arrangements had changed since the previous week when I left him there. We listened to the news and it referred to a number of Irishmen on board the ill-fated plane on its way to Brussels.

I then realised the time I had felt Peace coincided with Michael's death.

The sensation of real Peace enabled me to keep going. It was a consolation in times of great loneliness and sadness. But looking back now, I sometimes wonder if I could not have done more in my work in Northern Ireland because of it. Could I have helped people more to understand the true meaning of peace? Could I have taught that true peace comes only from inside ourselves? It is not something that can be achieved by political means. It requires tolerance and total acceptance of the 'other'. Peace has to be in the hearts and minds of people. I remember some years ago, when Drumcree was at its most difficult, hearing a woman from the Garvaghy Road saying in a radio interview that she thought the Orange march should be allowed to take its traditional route down the Garvaghy Raod, as it did not take long and the residents could ignore it. It seemed to me that this woman had a tolerance which people on both sides of the conflict could learn from. Maybe she also had peace of mind.

Can Peace be taught? I do not think so. But what can, hopefully, be taught is a way out of the sectarianism and hatred. It will take much time and patience. It will mean teaching people to think differently about their past, maybe letting go of the past, and to think differently of the 'other'. Ignorance, poverty and generations of unemployment, breed hatred and sectarianism. We see it happening in different parts of the world, most recently in Sighthills estate in Glasgow where the death of a Kurd, Firsat Yildiz Dag, followed by a knife attack on a young Iranian, can be traced to the young people in this deprived area growing up in a culture of social exclusion and violence. They have nothing and when they see asylum seekers coming into their estate and having their flats repaired and decorated they rebel. They do not know, nor are they told, that many of these people have come from horrific experiences in the countries they have fled from. They also do not know that the asylum seekers survive on vouchers and small cash handouts that amount to only seventy percent of their own income support.

As hatred and sectarianism grow more intense in Northern Ireland we must be aware of the reasons behind it. Why has hatred and sectarianism grown stronger as the Peace Process progresses? I think fear is the answer, fear of change, fear of the unknown, fear of the 'other'. A fear that largely comes from ignorance and is the enemy of Peace.

Think not forever of yourselves, oh Chiefs, nor of your own generation. Think of continuing generations of our families, think of our grandchildren and of those yet unborn, whose faces are coming from beneath the ground.

Founder of the Iroquois Confederacy
circa. 1000 AD

Sins of Omission
David Trimble

David Trimble serves as First Minister for the devolved government in Northern Ireland created after the Good Friday Agreement. He is a recipient of the Nobel Peace Prize.

L ast November, I took part in a ceremony marking the unveiling of a peace and reconciliation statue in the grounds of Stormont. The event was attended by representatives from across the spectrum of peace groups and organisations, as well as by politicians and representatives of the Israeli, German and Japanese governments. All were united in their abhorrence of conflict and solemn in reaffirming their desire to remember, and thereby prevent.

A few months earlier, while on a trip to Israel, I laid a wreath at the Holocaust Memorial at Yad Vashem and another at a cemetery to British war dead, also in Jerusalem. I had expected that the experience would be a poignant one and some of the more stark images have remained with me. Occasions such as these prompt the obvious questions.

What turns human beings into beasts? What happens within the human mind to make it possible to inflict death, injury and suffering on others just because they may look differently, speak differently or think differently?

There are no simple answers. But I would suggest that often the fault lies more with sins of omission.

Those who ask why wars happen, and why hatreds fester, should be reminded of Burke's warning that the conditions for the triumph of evil exist when *"good men {or people who should know better} do nothing"*. It is a mistake to take liberty for granted. The last major war of the 20th century was fought principally in its defence. I regard it as a privilege to be a citizen of a modern western European democratic society. And as custodians of democracy, all citizens have a duty to be vigilant in defending its interests by both word and deed.

For as the 18th century German philosopher, Immanuel Kant, suggested: *"The state of peace among men living side by side is not the natural state; the natural state is one of war"*.

Democracy may not be a perfect political system, but it is the fairest mankind has come up with so far and we disregard it at our peril.

Throughout the course of history, wherever community has risen against community and nation against nation, the same toxic brew of human failings has been to blame - whatever the publicly stated territorial excuse at the time.

In spite of the gloss or 'spin' applied, the root causes usually have included intolerance, mistrust, ignorance, prejudice, false perceptions, irredentism…

The Northern Ireland Troubles were perpetuated by at least some of those human weaknesses in greater or lesser measure. And there were plenty of people on both sides of the political divide who should have known better.

The Belfast Agreement seeks to recognise and address the causes of our conflict.

It has drawn a line through an old quarrel and has created instead a new set of relationships within our society, between north and south, and between Britain and Ireland.

Through devolution we have also been given the opportunity to foster a new relationship with the outside world. Seamus Mallon and I demonstrated this recently when we were received by President Chirac in Paris, and by Foreign Minister Fischer in Berlin, as part of a marketing campaign in Europe.

What was significant was that, as First Minister and Deputy First Minister, we were able to represent the interests of all of our people to foreign governments at the highest level. Northern Ireland is able to speak for itself now on the world stage.

There is a sense that we are moving into a more positive and peaceful era. We will still have problems, but the political structures are there for dealing with them. The political process is a good deal more robust than many people think. It will survive.

We are looking to the future as two communities, working in partnership.

The devolved administration is committed to the creation of an inclusive society in which everyone will have the chance to realise their full potential, regardless of class, colour or creed.

This contract with society, safeguarded by European human rights legislation, could have wider implications as Northern Ireland's prosperity continues to grow.

The prospects of, one day, requiring immigrant workers to fill posts in our high streets, offices and shop floors may not be as far-fetched as it might seem. The economic renaissance of the Republic of Ireland has seen just such a development.

Northern Ireland's transition to a more broadly based society would bring with it benefits and challenges. Benefits, because exposure to other cultures would be a good thing, and challenges because we would have to learn to accommodate other traditions and belief systems and guarantee them the same freedoms and tolerances that we enjoy.

In some senses it is Northern Ireland's misfortune that it is a small country right on the outer edge of Europe and separated from that continent by water. People don't pass through here en route to anywhere else. They stop with us only if they have business to do, or leisure time to spend.

As a result we have never enjoyed the educational influence experienced by other regions where there is a steady flow of cosmopolitan traffic.

When I am asked what peace is, I have to confess it is not a simple concept to quantify.

Is it the absence of violence? There is violence in every society.

Is it the absence of dissension? History contains no references to a civic society in which everyone thought in exactly the same way.

My understanding of 'peace' would be in terms of a democratic community at ease with itself, in which the natural tensions are recognised, in which difference is accommodated, and in which the stresses and strains of human co-existence are accounted for through agreed coping mechanisms.

A peaceful society is not one where crime or violence is absent; not one devoid of differences of opinion; but one where the rights of the individual are balanced by the responsibilities of the individual, and where diversity is not just tolerated, but celebrated.

Essential to its maintenance and stability is a shared understanding of, and support for, the institutions of law and order.

It has been said that ' the pen is mightier than the sword, but no match for a gun'. I would contend that events in Northern Ireland over the past thirty years have disproved that.

Terrorism and civic strife did not advance political change. The violence actually retarded it. The pace of change would have been much more rapid if terrorism had not intervened.

The gun and the bomb achieved nothing except to justify and entrench old mindsets more deeply.

Now that the primacy of politics has been re-established, it is appropriate that a peace and reconciliation memorial has been placed within the grounds of Stormont.

It is a daily reminder to us all that the only solution to Northern Ireland's problems lies fairly and squarely in the hands of its people, through the institutions of the Assembly and the Executive.

We, as a people, have the opportunity to re-build together, as equals. And after thirty violent, wasted years, there is an awful lot of catching up to do.

The Third Way:
Through the Wandering Rocks
Brendan O'Regan

*This article was originally printed in 'The Crane Bag' publication in
1984 with very generous help from Dr. Mark Patrick Hederman.*

W hen Ulysses was returning from Troy on the hazardous journey
home to Ithaca, he was faced at one point with a difficult decision
about his best way forward. On the one hand he could try to pass between
the sheer rock-faced cliff of the Scylla and the deadly whirlpool known as
Charybdis, or he could try to make his way through the wandering rocks.
These 'Wandering Rocks' must have been some kind of archipelago which
gave the optical illusion that the islands it comprised were floating and
constantly crashing into each other. The idea of a way forward between the
perils of the three motifs of sheer steadfast rock, restless whirlpools and
wandering rocks can be used symbolically to illustrate the direction I am
trying to point towards in this article.

The way forward, as I see it, in Northern Ireland, in Britain, in Europe, in
America, in the Third World - wherever - is similar for all of us and is
threatened by perils of all three varieties. The sheer rock face of Scylla is
the way of hard dogmatic facts, ideologies and creeds; the whirlpool of
Charybdis is the way of protest, whether that be the protest of the pacifist
or the terrorist. In the present state of world affairs, it seems to me that
both these ways have been tried and found wanting. We are forced to turn
back and try the third way.

The Third Way

It is this third way, symbolised by the Wandering Rocks, which I would like to describe in this article. Our most vivid mythological account of it is provided in Jason's search for the Golden Fleece. He sent a dove to show the way. The dove chose its moment carefully before flying through the clashing rocks. It got through, losing only the tip of its tail. The argonauts followed its example. They bided their time, waited for the right moment and then passed through unscathed but for some minor damage to the stern of the Argo. I think we have something to learn from this third approach to the treacherous journey forward and, without wishing to labour the parable, I would say that for me the 'wandering rocks' are made up of misunderstanding, distrust, fear and hate. The dove has always been a symbol of peace and once that messenger has been sent ahead, once the decision to go forward has been made, it is possible that many of these obstacles will reveal themselves as optical illusions. If we bide our time and choose the right moment for making our move we could find these rocks dissolving in the very ferment created by our determination to get through in spite of them.

The idea is a very simple equation. It is that peace depends primarily on self-interest. Self-interest relates to standard of living. When we accept this equation and realise that both are achieved by trust and co-operation in the economic, social and cultural fields, between those who are at loggerheads, whether on this island or at an international level, then we will begin to work realistically and effectively for peace.

At the moment there does exist a kind of co-operation based on self-interest between those who are otherwise divided by race, creed or political bias. However, this kind of endeavour is qualitatively different to what is here envisaged. The kind and scale of co-operative effort needed is only now made possible by two unparalleled and comparatively recent phenomena: the first is the threat of universal terrorism coupled with the possibility of global annihilation and the realisation that what we are working for now is not just prosperity but survival and the second is the extraordinary progress which mankind has made, particularly in the last fifty years, in the areas of technology and management. These two facts give an impetus and proficiency to the whole notion of co-operation which change its nature and its scope so radically that it might be less confusing to simply call it by some other name. These two new elements in our situation are also linked together. In our time mankind has succeeded in radically transforming the world, mostly as a result of war or the concentrated effort to make ourselves stronger than some identifiable adversary. The techniques used in these pursuits are those of scientific management both at the level of research and at the level of organisation; the coalescence of myriad minds for the implementation of perceived objectives. This skill in organising manpower has brought us technologically to a new threshold. In fact it has now become a cliché that technology has long since outstripped our capacity to control it. What is necessary, therefore, is that we employ these very same techniques and abilities to achieve the advance at a human level which will obviate the threats of terrorism, ever-increasing ethnic strife and the ever-present danger of nuclear warfare. So far we have failed to use the very same forces which have brought us to this technological brink to defeat these enemies which now threaten all mankind. Exactly the same kind of forces, the same management skills which allowed us to split the atom can and must now be deployed to protect us against the explosion of energy which the Manhattan Project unleashed as unlimited potential for either good or evil. We forget that it was the newly acquired human organisational technology and skills of management, linking together many thousands of scientific minds and organising these in terms of time, communication and resources which actually succeeded in splitting the atom. At another period in history, before the development of these management skills, a project of this complexity would have been unachievable, even if scientists as brilliant as Einstein had perceived that such a thing was possible. Now that we have developed these skills and techniques - mostly as a result of having to develop them through the sheer necessity and terror engendered by the wars of this century - it is now simply a question of switching these towards overcoming the human conflict problems which now threaten all humanity.

The switch can be made by a simple decision but one that must be taken at the highest level. It would be a decision like the one made by the President of the U.S.A. when America decided to put a man on the moon. That one decision brought together all those forces of scientific knowledge and administrative skills and provided these with the funds, the time and the equipment necessary to implement it. It is simply a question of recognising that mankind has the ability to achieve whatever the human mind can conceive, provided the resources are allocated to it.

It is essential that the commitment be given at the top to achieve any great purpose whether it be to split the atom or achieve world peace. When that commitment is given then energies are released and organisations formed to bring about the objective. Resources are made available which will allow people of ability to sit down day after day in an organised fashion to brainstorm the way forward towards their particular objective. In other words, what I am saying is that those very same forces which we brought together to split the atom can and must now be reassembled to reunite the atom. In this case I am referring to the individual human atoms which are in danger of global suicide unless some unifying power is released among them.

Such an achievement has already been accomplished on a large scale in Europe after the Second World War. Here the commitment was to never let this happen again, but the methods used to honour it were those of scientific management and economic co-operation, through the Marshall Plan, the Coal and Steel Community, the Organisation for European Co-operation and Development and now the European Economic Community. The strife and the differences which divided the members of this community were more deep-rooted and bitter than any that divide the superpowers of today, and, in some cases, they still exist. However, the human organisational structures and co-operative networks which have been elaborated over the years by Europeans allow such tensions to be absorbed into the body politic without becoming lethal or destructive of the whole.

The transformation which such a concerted effort can achieve, and has achieved, is not just a matter of economic endeavour and financial support. It is an acknowledged fact that when two or more people come together to co-operate for a common purpose, their mutual interplay starts a process of coalescence which results in a new combination like a chemical change. Groups of one kind or another begin to take shape and grow. No more striking example of this could be given than the remarkable rock concert which was held for famine relief in Africa in July of this year. The miracle of transformation which this combination of scientific management, technological skill and availability of human warmth and talent was able to achieve in one day is paradigm and proof of the powerful and dramatic forces which are at our disposal if only we begin to harness them effectively.

Teilhard de Chardin

In this regard Teilhard de Chardin was a prophet. Immediately after the first atomic bomb had exploded, de Chardin was able to say:

> *"Something wonderful has happened...At this crucial instance when the explosion was about to happen or not to happen, the first artificers of the atomic bomb were crouched on the soil in the desert. When they got to their feet it was over, it was mankind who stood up with them, instilled with a new sense of power."*

He claims that this power was qualitatively different from any previously experienced on this earth. There had been hints of it in the Palaeolithic age when fire was first invented, in the Neolithic age when agriculture was invented and in the industrial age when the energies of steam and electricity

246

were harnessed, but none of these brought about an 'essential change of plane'. The atomic explosion opened a door and raised mankind onto a new plane, not just because an apparently inviolable area of the universe had been penetrated but because:

> *"for the first time in history, through the non-fortuitous conjunction of a world crisis and an unprecedented advance in means of communication, a planned scientific experiment combining hundreds and thousands of trained minds had been successfully completed, and very swiftly. In three years a technical achievement had been realised which might not have been accomplished in a century of isolated efforts."*

De Chardin forecasts that such a combined task force, such a great co-operative human endeavour, should and could be employed to elaborate a programme of world peace for:

> *"in this as in other fields nothing in the universe can resist the converging energies of a sufficient number of minds sufficiently grouped and organized"*

De Chardin makes a very interesting observation from the biological point of view. Up to this point in history wars have been caused by man's desire for self-preservation. The very act of war implied the possibility of victory for one side or the other. The atomic age has completely undermined that age-old axiom and has reversed the situation: from now on self-preservation can only be achieved through peace. War, which used to be the weapon which ensured our freedom and our existence has now become the ultimate enemy and the unparalleled threat to survival.

"Everything that formerly made for war now makes for peace, and the zoological laws of conservation and survival must wear an opposite sign if they are to be applied to man. The whole phenomenon has been re-versed."

Organised Endeavour

What all this means is that we have to achieve peace or else be destroyed. Achieving peace is not going to happen through protest; it must be the result of an organised endeavour. In other words, the lessons we have learned and the methods we have elaborated through warfare must now be redirected to the goal of peace. Paradoxically we shall be using methods of warfare to achieve peace. Using the same energies and concentrated effort which were developed in us through the threat of war, to attack our enemies, we must now focus our attention on the recently created universal enemy which is warfare itself. We must declare war upon war.

The question then becomes how to organise such a co-operative endeavour for peace in ways similar to those used to split the atom or put a man on the moon? A most important point in this regard is the role of the state. The state controls a large proportion of the resources needed to launch any such project. This means in the first instance that the state would have to endorse a large scale plan to promote trust and co-operation through the direct machinery of government or through the semi-state organisations that handle commerce, industry, tourism and trade. Secondly, there is the whole field of private enterprise. Private enterprise is primarily activated by motives of self-interest. However, there are ways of offering incentives to private enterprise to open up new lines of communication using the machinery which they have for trade, commerce and tourism etc., to improve relationships between people. Thirdly, there is the need to encourage organisations outside of government which will help to relate people to people and promote trust and co-operation through the methods of organised management, linking together non-political forces in the communities that are in conflict. This third area, while it is non-political and of a voluntary nature, differs from the usual type of voluntary effort in that it has to be highly organised, applying methods of scientific management, research and organisation, so that it is, and is seen to be, a hard-nosed, realistic and practical endeavour and not just a 'do-good' romantic or overidealistic concept.

The weakness of the voluntary agency is that it lacks the continuity and stability of the government situation or the established business. People need security in order to commit themselves over a lengthy period to an ideal or purpose. The very creation of an organisation to achieve understanding, peace, trade and commerce, creates a power structure in itself which fights to preserve its own essential elements because it is in itself providing employment and a way of life for those who make it up. This can be seen in relation to the European integration. The ideal of finding a way forward out of post-war chaos through large scale co-operation between the nations of Europe would probably have died a long time ago were it not for the binding threads of the individual desires of those who were employed by Europe to ensure that the ideal succeeded.

The essential nature of this kind of progress through co-operation and the promotion of trust was endorsed by all the nations of East and West, together with the US and Canada, during the Helsinki Conference from 1975 to 1977, when programmes relating to social, economic and cultural co-operation were recognised by all those present as essential elements in building up peace and security. The momentum which it was hoped this conference might generate never got under way because of the conflict sustained by the great powers. However, the search for new methods of peace has reasserted itself and is symbolised by the decisions in the U.S.A. and Canada, in the latter part of 1984, to establish National Institutes of Peace. In the American case, a decision to allocate 16 million dollars from the Defence Department budget for this purpose is particularly significant, and in Canada the government's decision to allocate 7 million dollars in the next three years and 5 million dollars in each fiscal year thereafter to set up an International Peace and Security Institute in Ottawa, indicates the importance now attached to such thinking. It is also significant that an increasing number of universities on both sides of the Atlantic are planning courses in peace education and conflict resolution - a recognition by the higher institutes of learning that this is a whole new field of knowledge that needs to be developed and expanded.

There would seem to be little doubt that this recognition is gaining ground and becoming accepted in many places throughout the world. However, the implementation of such a new concept can be delayed, sometimes with disastrous consequences, simply because people are slow to accept what they regard as a new idea, unless it can be shown to have worked already in some comparable situation.

The Principal of 'Commensalism'

Here in Ireland, over the last six years, new ground has been broken and valuable experience has been gained in regard to methods of achieving peace by co-operation. Recognising that the conflict in Northern Ireland relates to the desire of the South to achieve unity with the North and the determination of the majority in the North to maintain the link with Britain, like-minded people on both sides of the border came together and set up Co-operation North. This organisation set itself the task of finding ways by which we could work together respecting our differences while at the same time realising that unless some way of overcoming these essential differences was found, we would be submerged by them. This co-operation has had to be achieved outside of government for reasons associated with the very nature of the conflict and so developed, out of necessity, a new non-political experiment in co-operation at the economic, social and cultural level and allied to the concept of scientific management outlined above. The experiment has achieved much but still has much more to achieve. A beginning has been made which, if sufficient moral and financial support is forthcoming, promises to lead to a successful end.

A difficulty with any such project is to find words to express it accurately without betraying its essential nature and without offending any of the parties in conflict who are always suspicious of the motivation and the goals of any such movement. Perhaps it is necessary to invent new words to describe the unique kind of relationship which an organisation like Co-operation North is trying to promote.

251

I am told that there is a term in biology called 'commensalism' which describes a kind of relationship in the animal world which comes somewhere between symbiosis, on the one hand, where the two partners in a relationship blend irretrievably into one another, and parasitism on the other, where one partner feeds shamelessly off the other. Commensalism, coming from the Latin word for a table (*mensa*), occurs when two or more animals live together but do not enter into any kind of physiological union. It shares a table, not a creed, an identity or a government; it harms no one and commits neither partner to anything more than an entirely pragmatic working agreement. The most striking example of this special kind of relationship is 'the Hermit Crab' who enters into commensal association with several other sea creatures for mutual protection, transport and food supply. This term and the relationship it describes would go along way towards a definition of the kind of co-operation which is here envisaged. It seems to me that such a relationship should be possible even in our present difficulties on this island. If even that most individualistic and autistic of creatures, the Hermit Crab, can engage in such relationships without losing his vocation as a hermit and his identity as a crab, then it must be possible for even the most intolerant nationalist and determined unionist to submit to such uncompromising and yet mutually beneficial links.

Co-operation North

A certain number of steps have already been taken in this direction. In the late 1970's a group of leaders in business, academic life, the trade unions, the professional bodies and voluntary organisations in Ireland, came together to co-operate in the economic, social and cultural areas, without any political strings attached. Co-operation North was established for this purpose in 1979. It was to act as a catalyst for companies, agencies, voluntary bodies and individuals from both parts of the island and thereby create a climate of mutual understanding and tolerance. The core of the organisation is formed by two private companies based in Belfast and Dublin with a common Board of Directors serving both companies. A full-time staff of ten operating from offices in Belfast and Dublin implement the organisation's programme.

In 1981 a private charity, Co-operation Ireland Inc., was established in the US to promote similar objectives and in London a support group was also formed in 1984 to support and raise funds for these ideas and activities. The European Commission takes a special interest in this work both by financial aid and by seconding a staff member as the organisations Chief Executive.

This recognition and support has not tempted Co-operation North to deviate from its non-political stand and objectives. Its programme remains at the economic, social and cultural level and in 1984 it brought together as many as 15,000 people and 2,000 groups both old and young and from differing political and religious persuasions.

However, without becoming political it is still necessary to go further than this and to increase the scale of this operation if any significant breakthrough is to come about in the near future. The time is ripe for an increased scale of co-operation in Ireland between North and South, using such outlets as tourism and industrial development, so as to provide greater employment and give a new image to both parts of the island without threat to either tradition.

To bring this about a number of approaches are presently being pursued by Co-operation North. An Irish Peace Institute has just been established the organism through which some of this increase in scale can be filtered. Its aim will be to promote fresh thinking in relation to peace-building and to sponsor initiatives which might help to achieve this aim. More specifically it has prompted a programme of co-operation between the University of Ulster and the National Institute for Higher Education in Limerick. This co-operation should help at many levels, especially in the area of research. It will also sponsor undergraduate and postgraduate studies in Peace and Conflict Resolution and develop open learning programmes and materials which might be of help to the eighty voluntary bodies in Ireland engaged in reconciliation work.

Research of this kind, leading to a number of publications, conferences and reports has already been pursued by the internationally recognised Centre for Conflict Studies at the University of Ulster since 1980. For this reason and also because of the successful and imaginative merger which it has succeeded in implementing between four different colleges which are now united into a sophisticated, pluralist and functionally orientated amalgam integrated into The University of Ulster, it was chosen as the ideal partner in the kind of co-operation which the Irish Peace Institute envisages.

The southern half of this same relationship stresses the technological and scientific management emphasis of the 'third way' outlined above. It was in the early 1970's that the Irish Government established the National Institute for Higher Education (NIHE) in Limerick to meet the growing need for higher education in the technological sphere. The aim was to produce graduates suitable for employment in an Ireland developed by international investment and committed to membership of the European Economic Community. The NIHE has since then developed into Plassey Technological Park where a range of public and private development organisations, research bodies and high technology companies are being attracted to the location, showing that state and private enterprise, Irish and foreign enterprise can successfully combine. The park is providing a national technological focus, improving the level of technology in existing Irish industry and commerce and creating around it an environment where future leaders of business, industry and the professions are being educated.

The combination of these two third-level institutes not only establishes an important link between the two parts of the island, one which can be developed even more by research and the practical implementation of the results of that research, but it also combines the various elements which make up the 'third way' towards peace already enumerated.

In international terms Ireland is a small island with a relatively small population on the periphery of Europe. There are clear advantages to be gained in promoting co-operation and trust between North and South and in co-ordinating our planning in areas such as tourism, energy, education, transport and communications. However, effective and long-term results demand a substantial and fully articulated programme which is continuous and unremitting. Such a programme implies organisation, planning, co-ordination in implementation and considerable resources. To be successful it needs funds and organisational resources made available at many different levels by government, by business, by trade unions and by voluntary organisations. It requires the deployment of up-to-date techniques of management and new methods of communication appropriate to the task. It merits as much professional skill as we devote, in both parts of Ireland, to promoting tourism and industrial development.

When the Argonauts got through the clashing rocks unharmed, we are told by Appollonius of Rhodes that the rocks were then rooted forever in one spot close to one another, for it had been decided by the Gods that this should be their fate if ever a human being saw them and sailed through. In Twentieth Century experience the Irish State is a prototype of democracy in practice which could become an effective laboratory and experiment helpful to other newly independent states emerging from a similar ex-colonial background. If we succeed in passing through these wandering rocks using the 'third way' of commensalism and co-operation, then the knowledge and experience gained from such a voyage would be of help to a world bedevilled now more than ever by terrorism and ethnic strife.

> *Pens of peace are mightier than the guns of strife,*
> *Writing, reading and sharing the treasures of life.*
> *Books spill wisdom and the rivers of plenty flow,*
> *Bullets spread death and the searing wind blow.*
> *Ballots bring a rule of love and guns a tale of tears,*
> *A mindless few to rule in a land of famine and fears.*